Beside the Ocean
of Time

Also by
George Mackay Brown

Poems
LOAVES AND FISHES
THE YEAR OF THE WHALE
FISHERMEN WITH PLOUGHS
POEMS NEW AND SELECTED
WINTERFOLD
SELECTED POEMS
VOYAGES
THE WRECK OF THE ARCHANGEL
SELECTED POEMS 1954–1983

Plays
A SPELL FOR GREEN CORN
THREE PLAYS
A CELEBRATION FOR MAGNUS

Novels
GREENVOE
MAGNUS
TIME IN A RED COAT
THE GOLDEN BIRD
VINLAND

Short Stories
A CALENDAR OF LOVE
A TIME TO KEEP
HAWKFALL
THE SUN'S NET
ANDRINA
THE MASKED FISHERMAN
THE SEA-KING'S DAUGHTER

Essays
AN ORKNEY TAPESTRY
LETTERS FROM HAMNAVOE
UNDER BRINKIE'S BRAE
ROCKPOOLS AND DAFFODILS

Non-fiction
PORTRAIT OF ORKNEY
LETTERS TO GYPSY

For Children
THE TWO FIDDLERS
PICTURES IN THE CAVE
SIX LIVES OF FANKLE THE CAT

Beside the Ocean of Time

GEORGE MACKAY BROWN

JOHN MURRAY

© George Mackay Brown 1994

First published in 1994
by John Murray (Publishers) Ltd.,
50 Albemarle Street, London W1X 4BD

Reprinted 1994

A catalogue record for this book is available
from the British Library

ISBN 0-7195-5368-7

Typeset in Linotron 11/14pt Times
by Rowland Phototypesetting Ltd.,
Bury St Edmunds, Suffolk
Printed and bound in Great Britain by
Butler & Tanner Ltd, Frome and London

Contents

The Road to Byzantium   1

Bannockburn   21

A Man's Life   47

Broch   71

The Muse   91

The Press-Gang and The Seal Dance   129

Aerodrome   179

Fisherman and Croftwoman   193

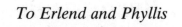

To Erlend and Phyllis

The Road to
Byzantium

OF ALL THE lazy useless boys who ever went to Norday school, the laziest and most useless was Thorfinn Ragnarson.

'I don't know what to do with you, you're useless,' said Mr Simon the teacher. 'I'll speak to your father.'

So Mr Simon met Thorfinn's father, Matthew Ragnarson, in the shop one Saturday morning. He said he was sorry he couldn't do much with Thorfinn. Try as he would, he didn't seem to succeed in teaching the boy anything.

On Friday morning, for example, he had been telling the class about the Norsemen in Constantinople 800 years ago – Thorfinn had sat there taking nothing in – he was watching a thrush on the wall outside, inattention personified – 'a dreamer,' said Mr Simon.

'He's no good at farm work either,' said Matthew the farmer. 'You'd think he'd be good at something – everybody has a gift of some kind, don't they? – but Thorfinn drifts about as idle as a butterfly.'

1

Isa Estquoy who kept the shop and post-office was listening like a little inquisitive mouse. That way, Isa got to know more about the island of Norday and its inhabitants than the minister or the doctor, even. She just listened to the customers, and gave an occasional squeak.

'An ounce of bogey roll and a box of matches,' said Matthew Ragnarson to Isa. 'And four bars of milk chocolate.'

'Maybe Thorfinn could join the army,' said Mr Simon.

'Not a hope,' said the farmer. 'He would be shot at dawn for falling asleep on guard. He would wander away behind enemy lines and be shot there as a spy. Everything Thorfinn does is a mistake, somehow.'

'He's a nice boy, Thorfinn,' said Isa Estquoy in a little tiny voice like a mouse. 'He's not like some of the other boys, stealing sweeties off the counter. Some of them threw a squib into the shop last Halloween! Rainbow my cat nearly died of fright. I know the names of the young scoundrels. Thorfinn isn't in the list. Thorfinn's a good boy.'

'A tin of oxtail soup and a book of three-ha'penny stamps,' said Mr Simon in his schoolroom voice. Mr Simon was a solitary man and looked after himself.

'No,' squeaked Isa Estquoy. 'Oh no, Mr Simon. You owe five pounds three shillings and fivepence, it's all marked here against you in the book. I'm sorry, I can't serve you till the account is settled.'

'You'll be paid when I get my salary at the end of the month!' thundered Mr Simon, and his face flushed a little, because some other women customers had come into the village shop.

'I hope so indeed,' chirped Isa, handing over the tin of soup and the book of stamps. 'In this island people always pay for what they buy, on the nail.'

2

Mr Simon went out, red in the face.

'The trouble is,' said Isa to her customers, 'he has to keep a divorced wife and three bairns in Glasgow. Well, that's his lookout. He should have thought twice before he married her. But I'm sure the fault is all his. A bully. Did you hear the way he shouted just now? But he won't frighten me. If he doesn't settle his bill at the end of the month I'll write to the school authorities in Edinburgh.'

The island women discussed Mr Simon for a time. One, Bella Simpson, thought he was stern, maybe, but a good teacher. One, Tina Lyde, thought he was very good-looking and needed somebody to look after him in the schoolhouse. One thought he was visiting the village inn too often, but then Mabel was the weekend barmaid there, and Mabel had a way of attracting customers. Mr Simon often had hangovers, that's why he was often in a bad mood.

Isa Estquoy squeaked with mirth.

Matthew Ragnarson put his tobacco in his pocket and left the shop.

'Poor Matthew,' said Tina Lyde who had a soft spot for every unmarried man in the universe, 'he could do with some well-handed woman up at Ingle, to bring up his four bairns, the three lasses and Thorfinn . . .'

Matthew the farmer walked along the two-mile road to Ingle.

His three daughters, Inga, Sigrid, and Ragna came running to meet him. He gave them each a bar of chocolate.

'Where's your brother?' said Matthew. 'He's usually first in the queue when the chocolate's being handed out.'

Inga and Sigrid and Ragna waved vaguely here and there. Thorfinn their brother could be anywhere – on the far side of the hill, down on the shore with the cormorants

3

and Jimmo Greenay the beachcomber, in some hovel listening to old folk telling moth-eaten stories.

*   *   *

As a matter of fact, Thorfinn at that very moment was on a Swedish ship, the *Solan Goose*, anchored off a port in the Baltic. The skipper, Rolf Rolfson, was making plans to meet the prince of Rus, with a view to trading with his people and establishing good relations.

It should be said that Thorfinn was actually in the barn of Ingle, lying curled in the bow of his father's fishing yole, with the collie Stalwart sleeping in the stern. But in his imagination he was walking up a beach in the eastern Baltic, along with six other Swedish vikings, to meet a troop of envoys from the court of Rus.

Each Swede had a hand hovering not too far from the axe in his belt.

'We greet you, friends!' cried Thorfinn, a bit of a quaver in his voice.

'Shut up!' said Rolf Rolfson. 'I'll do the talking. Leave it to me.' The Russians stood now on the bank above the beach. They held up hands of peace, palm outward, to the Swedes.

Rolf ordered three heavy cases of iron ore to be set down on the stones, a gift to the prince of Rus from the Swedish merchants.

'One of you stay beside the small boat,' said Rolf Rolfson. 'Be ready to make a quick dash for it in case they try any funny stuff.'

The seven Russians clapped their hands with delight over the open boxes of Swedish iron ore. A huge man lifted a lump of ore and balanced it in his hand. He nodded. 'He must be a blacksmith, that one,' said Rolf.

The young Prince Boris seemed to be delighted with his guests.

The prince and his court lived in a little palace not far from the sea. There was a village of wooden huts and gardens beside the palace. It seemed to be a splendid palace, all ivory and marble and oak, but when Thorfinn got inside it was filthy and smoky and grease-smelling, and the rain came in.

At night the Swedes were given bearskins to cover themselves.

'Now,' said Boris the prince, 'you will stay here forever, my friends, and eat the fat of the land.'

They ate pieces of roasted wolf and bear, and the ale was so strong that Thorfinn nodded off where he sat, after two mouthfuls; and he had to jerk himself into wakefulness.

Though cobwebs draped the rafters, there was now a magnificent silver salver on the table with a boar's head on it.

'We will be careful in our dealings with this Boris,' said Rolf Rolfson to his men. 'Drink no more than one horn of his beer. Generosity can go too far.'

Later Rolf Rolfson said to Thorfinn, 'You, Orkney boy, stand guard at the door of our room. Rouse us if you hear anything suspicious.'

Thorfinn stood for four nights at the door of the chamber.

At midnight on the fourth night he heard the young prince in talk with his chief bodyguard, an immense man with a beard as brown as a bear, called Illyich. Lantern light splashed them as they talked in the yard.

'Listen well, Illyich,' Prince Boris was saying. 'Tomorrow night, we are to make a feast for the Swedes.

Set a big barrel of the strongest ale beside the fire. The Swedes will get drunk one after the other and fall asleep at their benches. Then you and your men, Illyich, will send them on the longest journey they can ever take . . . Phew! – the servant women will mop up the blood in the morning. Then their ship, the *Solan Goose*, will be mine. It is a fine ship. I can sail in her to China or Greenland.'

'I will do what you want,' said Illyich in his deep rich voice. And he laughed.

Thorfinn shook Rolf Rolfson awake and told him the midnight talk he had just heard.

'Well done, boy,' said the skipper. 'I am looking forward to this feast.'

In the morning Rolf told the other Swedes what was afoot. He told them to bring their daggers, hidden under their shirts, to the feast. He warned them not to drink any of the strong ale, merely to froth their beards with it, so that the prince would think they were drinking deeply. Secretly each man must pour the beer into the earthen floor.

That night when they were all seated on the benches, a man went round filling their ale-horns, and there was a high fleece of froth on every horn. The Swedes let on to drink deeply but they only laced their beards with froth, like men on a spume-flung voyage. Thorfinn had no beard – being a boy – but he had a cluster of tiny bubbles round his mouth. Dogs lapped the pools of beer on the floor.

'Drink deeply,' cried Prince Boris. 'It is my best ale. It is ten years old. You will sleep well this night, my friends. Far, far you will venture into realms unknown.'

Secretly, the Swedes poured their ale into the earthen floor. Two drunken hounds rolled their eyes as if the world was a crazy place and went lolloping over to the fire and unrolled long red smoking tongues and went to sleep.

Three men came in and one had a harp of mammoth tusk, and they began to sing. They sang in such powerful deep voices that Rolf was unable to converse with his men.

'When the boar's head is brought in,' said Rolf, 'that will be the sign. We will turn ourselves into wild boars and we will have the boars' revenge on those boar-hunters who have killed a thousand boars since their grandfathers first hunted tuskers and grunters in the forest.'

'Drink deeply, friends,' cried Boris. 'The best of the beer is to come.'

The music went on.

Rolf said to Boris, 'I thought this was a feast you had invited us to. That seems to be death music that the musicians are playing.'

'It is music of the hunt,' said Boris. 'Fill the horns of our guests. Don't you hear the cries of the wild swine in the forest? That's what the music is about. Surely you hear the boar's cry of defiance to the hunters and the dogs. It is all in the music.'

The dark chant went on and on.

'Enough now!' cried Prince Boris. 'Bring in the boar's head.'

As soon as the boar's head, reeking, was carried in from the kitchen on the magnificent silver platter, Rolf gave a sign and the Swedes took out their daggers and before the wolf outside had stopped howling not one man of the palace was alive, except Boris the prince and the harpist.

There was a great lamentation of women in the village.

Boris stood there, amid all the carnage, and he said to

Rolf, 'You're a cleverer man than I thought, Swede. You will go far, Rolf Rolfson. A man can go so far, as far as he has it in him to go, then even the luckiest man must lie down under a stone.'

'Don't kill the harpist,' said Rolf. 'He is a talented man. That was a good elegy he made, even before the death. A pity if such a good musician were to die too soon.'

So the prince and the musician went out under the stars, and nothing was ever heard of them again.

It was later said that in the Ural mountains in the east there was a travelling musician, who was accompanied everywhere by a young ragged man. And those two gave half of all the money they earned to the beggars and blind folk they met on the way. Before he played in any village square, the musician would kneel before the melancholy young man, his companion, and say, 'Prince, may this music I am going to play now sound well in your ears . . .' Those two wanderers were said to be Prince Boris and his harpist.

Rolf Rolfson took over that country but after two years he became tired of tax-gathering and boar-hunting and staying in one place.

He had a hundred men carry the *Solan Goose* across a great tract of land to the banks of a river called the Volga.

Rolf said to his helmsman Grettir, 'Grettir, you are to stay behind and be prince here in Rus now. Make wars and treaties east and west, become the king of a mighty kingdom. May your name resound down the ages, Grettir.'

Grettir said all he wanted to do was to sit at the steering-oar of the *Solan Goose*, and so at last come home, an old man, and die in Sweden.

'Your stars are not written that way, Grettir,' said Rolf, 'but as I have said.'

So Grettir watched sadly as the *Solan Goose* set sail down the wide River Volga. Then he went back to his palace at the edge of the forest.

There, that summer, he married a beautiful woman, and they were prince and princess of that region.

The *Solan Goose* was all summer sailing down the Volga. Thorfinn didn't think there could be such a long wide river in the world.

Sometimes, out of a black forest fringing the river, a shower of arrows would come swooping into the ship. One oarsman, Valt, was killed. Rolf Rolfson told his crew to set up the shields.

Sometimes the forests thinned out and they saw immense plains, with sheep grazing and a shepherd boy playing a pipe. The boy seemed to be quite unafraid of the strange ship. He sat and played on his pipe . . . The shepherd dog came down to the river shore and barked against them.

Many weeks' sailing down the river, the lookout men sighted early in the morning an orchard. Every tree was laden with apples and pears.

'I have a great longing,' said Rolf the skipper, 'to sink my teeth into a ripe red apple. We will go ashore and get some.'

Thorfinn felt the inside of his own mouth running and rilling with desire for the fruit.

So the *Solan Goose* dropped anchor and half a dozen men rowed ashore in the little coracle.

Thorfinn begged to be taken with them.

There was a little village beside the orchard. When the

villagers saw the strange vessel hesitating and halting on the river, they ran away among the trees – men and women, old doddering people, children, dogs and geese and cats.

The Swedes plucked several baskets of fruit from the trees.

Thorfinn sank his teeth into an apple. At once his mouth gushed with freshness and sweetness! He had to draw his breath before the next bite.

Solmund, one of the crew, said they ought to set the orchard on fire. A burning orchard would be a sight to wonder at.

'You're a fool, Solmund,' said Rolf. 'Even if it could be done, we wouldn't do it.'

The sailors laughed.

'Well,' said Solmund, a little downcast, 'at least we can burn down the village.'

But Rolf said they wouldn't put torches to the village either.

Instead, Rolf took a large silver coin from his pouch and laid it on the sill of the largest house there. 'We will pay those people for their excellent fruit,' he said.

Then they rowed back to the *Solan Goose*.

The men gorged themselves on the apples and pears. Solmund ate so much that he had to lean over the side and be sick.

The sailors laughed.

They raised anchor and floated downstream.

Before they turned a bend in the river, Thorfinn looked back and saw the villagers standing in the doors of their houses.

A dog barked at the disappearing ship, but it seemed to Thorfinn to be barks of joy.

An old man was holding up his hand. His fingers flashed like a star . . .

The baskets of apples lasted them a full week. The fruit made a pleasant change from the great river fish they were always eating, sturgeon.

'I will never eat a fish again, so long as I live!' grumbled Solmund.

Sometimes one of the sailors called Bjorn who was a fowler back home at Sollentuna in Sweden brought down a few wild geese that were flying between two clouds. Then the stewpot bubbled over the fire amidships.

'Oh,' said Rolf, 'for a taste of good bread! I think often of the warm crusted loaves my mother bakes in Gothenburg.'

But they did not taste bread for months.

The land on either side of the river broadened into fertile pasture and wheatlands as they sailed south.

Rolf had an eye like an eagle. 'I see a mill beside a little stream over there,' he said. 'I think with luck we may be eating bread for our supper. We will go ashore now and have a word with the miller.'

They got into the coracle and rowed ashore with a few sacks to hold the grain.

The fields of golden corn stretched back to the low hills, mile on mile of fertility. Many inland villages must have lived off that plain.

They saw the miller at the top door of his mill. First the miller let fly a spear at the Swedes. It stuck quivering in the ground at Rolf's feet. Then the miller put a horn to his mouth, and blew so hard Thorfinn thought the man's cheeks would burst.

No sooner were the last echoes of the horn dying away than they heard the sound of hooves on the hard earth.

11

Over the ridge rode a score of horsemen, urging on the horses, waving swords. The swords made flashing circles in the sun.

'Now,' said Solmund, 'that miller certainly deserves to have his mill burned about his ears.'

'Save your breath to get back to the ship,' said Rolf.

The Swedes ran down to the shore.

The Cossacks' horses pranced on the river bank above.

Thorfinn stumbled on a stone and fell.

'Hurry!' shouted Rolf.

Thorfinn heard footsteps on the loose stones. He could almost feel the hot breath of a Cossack on his neck. Then he was up and off like an otter. He had to swim to catch up with the coracle. He was dragged, streaming cold water, into the little wicker boat.

'That was a near thing,' said Rolf.

'They'd have had you for their breakfast, the Cossacks,' said Solmund.

The sailors laughed.

Now the river bank was lined with a score of Cossacks on horseback.

The miller seemed to be dancing with joy at the door of his mill.

All at once the Cossacks began to sing. Such a deep magnificent chorus Thorfinn was never to hear again in his lifetime. It seemed that the rich steppe itself had given voice.

'I think we won't be tasting bread now till we get to Byzantium,' said Rolf the skipper.

At last the river emptied itself into a great sea.

The sailors sniffed the salt with joy.

'It's called the Black Sea,' said Rolf. 'It isn't really

a sea at all, like the Atlantic. It's just a biggish pond among sand-dunes, like our own Baltic. Turn the rudder west.'

On the tenth day they sighted the domes and palaces of Byzantium.

'One of two things will happen to us here,' said Solmund. 'Either they'll make us slaves and we'll go rattling with chains to our graves, or else the Emperor will enrol us in his guard.'

A very official-looking launch came to meet them. It was like a hedgehog, that vessel, with the spears and axes and swords of the men who manned her.

The commander shouted a few words – a greeting or a warning – to the *Solan Goose*.

Rolf replied, speaking in his Norse tongue.

At once the commander ordered his soldiers to sheathe their weapons. The ships drifted alongside. The commander put his hand on the thwart and leapt lightly aboard the *Solan Goose*.

He put his arms about Rolf Rolfson and embraced him.

Solmund giggled. 'Better that than an embrace of iron chains,' he said.

Rolf appeared confused for a moment at being hugged, this way and that, with crossed necks. Then he gave the commander a sturdy thump on the shoulder. (Thus the men of the north greet one another.)

Before the end of the week, after many interviews with officials and the filling in and filing of many documents, Rolf and his sailors were led through a door of the imperial palace.

Once or twice that day, Thorfinn wondered if he had died and was in paradise.

But then, in the courtyard, he saw blind men and

crippled men begging for alms. Their wounds suppurated and flies feasted on their sores.

Rolf Rolfson had brought gifts from the king of Sweden to the Emperor. The presents were graciously received and borne away by officials. There seemed to be thousands of bureaucrats in the palace.

The men of the *Solan Goose* didn't actually cast eyes on the eastern emperor for many weeks.

First they were invited to have a bath – so hot that Solmund cried out that they were being boiled alive, like lobsters. Then the splendid uniform of the Emperor's own guard, the Varingers, was spread out for them. (The Emperor always insisted that his élite guard must be recruited from Scandinavia: they were the most trustworthy men in the world, and the greatest swordsmen.)

A rather smaller uniform had to be found for Thorfinn Ragnarson from Orkney.

A great supper was set for them: eggs and dolphins' fins and young eaglets, and goblets of sweet wine, and fruits that, once tooth-broken, dropped nectar down the throat.

The men ate heartily. They were avid for good food after the monotonous river diet of sturgeon and wild geese.

'And yet,' said Rolf Rolfson, 'I think the most toothsome thing I have eaten tonight is that hot crisp loaf. The baker here must be a magician.'

That night they slept in beds of soft down, a long dreamless sleep between Europe and Asia.

But next night, and every night as long as they were in Byzantium, they slept in their permanent quarters, the barracks. There the beds were of hard boards and their blankets were goatskins.

Solmund complained about that.

'Quite right,' said Rolf Rolfson. 'Soldiers have to live rough and be ready for anything.'

Their main rations thereafter were bread and cheese, olives and beer, with fish and meat at the weekends. One day a week they were doled out water and oatcakes only, iron rations.

The guardsmen from Norway and Denmark who had been in the Emperor's service for years, welcomed the newcomers, some grudgingly, some wholeheartedly.

They had many mutual acquaintances in the Baltic and the North Sea.

A monkey dressed in the uniform of the Varingers came ambling into the barracks. It swung from a rafter and gibbered at the new recruits.

'An insult, putting a thing like that among us!' said Solmund.

'He'll bring us luck,' said Rolf.

The monkey, called Hieronymus, sat often on Thorfinn's shoulder.

After two months of regimentation, Rolf Rolfson's men began to be bored.

'We wouldn't care to stay here for ever,' they said.

Solmund said, 'I want to get back sometime to Sweden to see my wife Hild and our little son.'

Rolf said, 'You know it is impossible for us ever to return to Sweden. The king outlawed us for killing his casteelan in Munkfors and rifling the treasury there.'

They all agreed that they would be killed if they set foot on the shore of Sweden again.

'And yet we are tired now of all the sun and gold and emerald here in Byzantium,' said Rolf. 'It can never be ours. We must rot into old age as best we can.'

15

Word was brought that a band of Turks had stormed one of the Emperor's outposts.

'Get ready,' said Rolf. 'I think we will see some fighting soon against the Turks.'

But the Varingers who had been a long time in the barracks and the palace laughed. 'We don't fight,' they said. 'The mercenaries do the fighting. We are here to guard the Emperor.'

A whole summer passed. The Varingers drilled. They played dice and chess. They got drunk on wine at weekends and fought with each other. The citizens, who were often hungry and always poor, spat at any solitary Varinger they met on the street, then ran off before the guardsman could strike out with his baton.

Thorfinn longed more and more for the green hills and blue waters of Orkney.

Never once did the crew of the *Solan Goose* see the Emperor Manuel. The emperor was embowelled deep in the ivory and gold and silk of the palace. Or he walked with his courtiers in a hidden walled garden, with lutes and flutes playing, and ladies fluttering fans like butterflies.

One day there seemed to be great excitement down at the waterfront. Crowds were streaming along the street outside the barracks, going down to the wharf.

'I hope,' said a grizzled old Dane who had been a Varinger for thirty years and would never see Elsinore again, 'that it isn't another troop of Crusaders. There's always bad trouble when the Crusaders come. The dregs and scum and layabouts of Europe, most of them.'

But soon they knew that ten ships from Orkney had anchored in the strait, and permission had been given to Earl Rognvald of Orkney and Bishop William of Orkney

16

and the eight other skippers to be received by the emperor.

The earl and the bishop had salt in their beards, and their eyes were crinkled with Mediterranean sun and sea-glitters. They acknowledged the cheers of the towns-people and threw handfuls of silver coins. Then the townspeople gave them a louder greeting still.

Earl Rognvald and his company passed along the ranks of the Varingers. The Earl looked keenly at every face as he went past. He stopped before Thorfinn Ragnarson and said, 'What's a young Orkney farm boy doing here in Byzantium?'

Thorfinn stammered out that he had run away from home two years before because everyone on his island kept saying he was an idle useless boy.

'I know your father who farms in Norday,' said Earl Rognvald. 'He is missing you greatly. So are the little sisters. I will see what I can do. Have patience.'

Then the earl and bishop and the commanders were received with fanfares into the great palace. Voice after voice inside intoned, 'Earl Rognvald of Orkney and Bishop William of Orkney,' each voice seeming to be a fading echo of the last as the procession penetrated ever deeper into the palace, and came at last to the throne room where the Emperor Manuel sat on his golden throne.

A silver trumpet thrilled.

'Well,' said Rolf Rolfson in the barracks that night, 'here we are, famous Vikings and adventurers, and who does the earl speak to but our cabin-boy.'

Then the crew of the *Solan Goose* began to throw dice on the wine-stained tables.

And a few of them whispered that soon now they would

steal down by night to where the *Solan Goose* was moored and sail away, for this life of idleness was beginning to gnaw at their nerves.

Rolf Rolfson told them not to be fools. The *Solan Goose* was no longer where they had left her. The wharfside thieves had stolen her a month since, and now she probably had a new name and a new crew and was trading somewhere between Greece and Africa.

'Resign yourselves,' said Rolf. 'We'll be here to the end of time. You can choose a little burial mound any day you like.'

At that, Solmund put his head in his folded arms and began to burble and weep.

'Pass round the wine-skin,' said Rolf. 'Tomorrow we get our wages.'

One day a month later Thorfinn, with Hieronymus the monkey on his shoulder, was sitting in a shady corner of the barracks, when a shadow fell on him. He looked up, and there stood Earl Rognvald of Orkney.

'Tomorrow,' said the earl, 'we are sailing away from Byzantium. The Emperor has asked us to stay on, but my people in Orkney and Shetland and Caithness have been without a governor for a long time – I must go back to them now.'

'Take me with you,' said Thorfinn. 'Please.'

The earl laughed. 'The music of your island speech,' he said, 'is more beautiful to me than all the treble and bass singers of the Mediterranean. Be down at the quayside at sunrise.'

'No,' said Thorfinn. 'For they will execute me for desertion.'

'I have spoken about you to the Emperor,' said Earl

Rognvald. 'He has given permission. Go and make ready. Tell nobody. You'll have to leave that monkey behind.'

Hieronymus chittered and spat at Earl Rognvald.

Next morning at reveille the Swedes woke and found Thorfinn Ragnarson's bed empty.

'The young fool,' said Rolf Rolfson. 'If the wharfside gangsters get a grip of him, he'll be dead before the first hair's on his chin. If the Emperor's police find him . . .' He drew his hand across his throat.

But even as Rolf spoke Thorfinn was on board the earl's ship *Saint Magnus* sailing west through the wine-dark waters of the Mediterranean.

Six months later he came ashore at Scapa, with seven silver pieces in his purse, a gift from Earl Rognvald.

A fisherman sailed him to the island of Norday. There he had a good reception from his father and three sisters.

Thorfinn Ragnarson was held in high esteem on account of his adventure.

'He wasn't such a fool after all, that boy,' said the three old women who met every morning beside the village well.

*   *   *

Thorfinn woke up from his dream of the Volga and Byzantium, humped in the bow of his father's yole. He surfaced slowly through eight and a half centuries.

He heard his sister Ragna's voice from the yard. 'Where are you, Thorfinn? It's teatime.'

And Sigrid mocked, 'You're a lazy idle useless boy.'

Bannockburn

WHAT A BORING day it had been in Norday school!

Usually, Thorfinn liked history, sitting at home reading his history book under the paraffin lamp.

But Mr Simon took all the enchantment out of history, with his long lists of the kings of Scotland and the battles that Scotland had either magnificently won or been gloriously defeated in, together with their dates.

This litany had its climax in 1314, midsummer day, under Stirling Castle, at a place called Bannockburn, when King Robert the Bruce had shattered the great English army and so sealed Scotland's independence for ever.

But Mr Simon had a way of making that exciting story dull, too.

Mr Simon thwacked the blackboard with his pointer. Battle of Bannockburn 1314 was chalked on the blackboard.

'*Battle of Bannockburn 1314*,' chanted the school children of Norday, over and over.

It was as dull as ditchwater.

The entire day was a washout. After tea – a boiled egg and oatcakes – Thorfinn went with his father to the smithy where a few fishermen and crofters came in the evening to tell stories, or argue politics.

Jock Seatter the blacksmith was a very old man, but still strong and keen-eyed, and he delighted in the evening discussions. He would close down the forge and sit on the anvil, and fill his pipe. Much better that than spending the evening with Madeline his wife.

But on this particular night Jock Seatter was expecting Willum Holm's plough-horse, Troy, to be shod.

'You can all idle,' said old Jock Seatter to the village parliament sitting on the worn bench that occupied one wall, 'but my work is never done.'

He took a bag of peppermints (pandrops) from a niche in the wall and passed it round. He gave Thorfinn an extra pandrop.

Tonight the tide of their talk set towards politics. That, for Thorfinn, was always dreary.

Thomas Vass was a Liberal. 'Free trade,' said Thomas Vass the laird's factor. 'Free trade the world over, and there'll be no more wars, no, nor no more poverty neither. Let the fruits and inventions of earth be open to all the peoples. Then no country will be frightened of any other country. No barriers – no restrictions. There's the cure for the ills of the world – free trade . . .'

But Jimmo Greenay who was the poorest man in the island, beachcomber and rat-catcher, denied this. Jimmo was a Tory . . . 'Oh no no,' he said in a salt-rough voice, 'Oh never! The British Empire – the sun never sets on the British Empire. Where would we be, wanting the wealthy powerful men who've made Britain what she is today? We don't need foreigners and their goods. The goods we manufacture are better than anything France or Germany or America can produce. Keep their cheap trash out of Britain! Oh yes – I agree – we do have a work to do in the world – to civilize the millions of savages from China to Tierra del Fuego. Yes, and to keep the Irish in their place. The Conservatives will guide the ship of state through the stormiest waters!'

So spoke the poorest man in Norday, who was often glad enough to chew a raw whelk or a piece of seaweed.

Ben Hoy the retired ship's engineer was a socialist. 'The whole human race', Ben Hoy argued night after night, 'is poised for a great surge forward. I'm telling you men this, every man born has a great potential stored up in him. But it's never realised. The chains of poverty and ignorance are forever holding us back, I most solemnly assure you. Do you know this, men, what I'm going to tell you? – I've sailed the world over, I have, I've made a dozen salt circles of the globe, and I'm telling you, the world is a rich place, it's like a golden dripping honeycomb. Who gets all that sweetness?– a bunch of top-hatted capitalists, a few fops in the House of Lords whose ancestors climbed over the broken bodies of the poor to get to where they are. Oh yes, and newspaper owners and arms manufacturers and slum landlords. Get rid of that lot – nationalize the means of production and distribution – and then men and women the world over will be happy healthy fulfilled human beings, I assure you!'

The dozen men in the smithy considered this for a while. They filled their pipes, some cleaned their pipe-stems with seagull feathers, a few struck matches and blew clouds of bogey roll.

Jock Seatter looked out to see if Willum Holm was on the road with his horse Maggie.

Howie Ayre the quarryman said, 'No, I don't see that this socialism will work at all. If you gather all the money in this world in one heap and divide it out equally so everybody gets a share – it sounds fine, I know – but the canny hardworking folk, they'll slowly save and gather in, and the idle spendthrifts will scatter their share to the wind – yes, they'll drink and gamble it all away – and in the end we'll be back where we were. Human nature – you can't get past human nature . . . Socialism takes no account of that. What then?'

Simon Taing, the young innocent-eyed farmer of the Bu, said there was a simple solution. Just gather all the money together again – all the wealth of the world in one big mountain of silver and gold, and divide it once more into equal portions.

The men shuffled and snorted and cleared their throats. 'Greater rubbish I have never heard,' said Thomas Vass the factor seriously. And he shook his head.

Matthew Ragnarson, Thorfinn's father, never took part in those discussions. He just sat on his hands on the bench, and laughed sometimes, and smoked.

Mr MacTavish, the new proprietor of the inn, put his head round the door, and hoped he wasn't interrupting but he wanted a word with the blacksmith. Jock Seatter had to go close up to MacTavish so he could hear him properly (the smith had grown hard of hearing lately). 'Can you do wrought iron?' shouted the innkeeper in his Edinburgh voice. 'I want a new sign for the inn. Now, could you make me a lion rampant to hang over the door?'

'To be sure, to be sure,' said Jock Seatter. He wasn't quite sure what a lion rampant was, but he never turned down a job. 'I won't be able to do it till after the agricultural show, though. I'm just expecting Willum Holm and his horse. This is a busy time. Sit down, man. The bench is a bit dusty but it'll bear you up. Have a pandrop.'

So MacTavish the publican took his seat in the Norday parliament for the first time, and it wasn't long before he made his colours plain: he was a Scottish Nationalist.

Mr MacTavish spoke at great length – too long, most of the smithy-men thought – about the mighty nation Scotland had been before that disastrous union with England in 1707. 'We were a great people in the counsels of Europe,' he said. 'We had famous poets and sailors, and a language of our own – no, two languages, Gaelic and Lallans – because Scotland is a fusion of Gaels and Lowlanders. But all that glory was shorn away in 1707, except that we had our own laws and our Presbyterian kirk. We were a rump of England, nothing more. But even today, though Scotland is a poor oppressed nation, we still produce the greatest doctors, engineers, explorers that the world has ever known. And our education system – that's the envy of the world too.'

Ben Hoy objected that Orkney had never been a part of Scotland anyway till 1472 and then the Scots had fallen on the once powerful earldom of Orkney and battened on it like hoodie crows. Terrible it had been.

MacTavish brushed that aside. 'Well,' said he, 'you've been Scottish now for a long time. That's an old song you're singing, my man.'

MacTavish smoked cigarettes, little white acrid-reeking cylinders, one after the other, and the smoke seemed to drive him to more eager eloquence still. He recited a litany of names – Mary Queen of Scots, Bonny Prince Charlie, John Knox, James Watt, David Livingstone, David Hume, William Wallace, King Robert the Bruce.

If only Mr MacTavish had lived in those days – how gladly would he have followed the troops converging on the little torrent, the Bannock Burn, under Stirling Castle!

Thorfinn closed his eyes and leaned his head on his father's shoulder. The inn-keeper's voice went on and on.

*   *   *

A knight on horseback and a boy were riding through Sutherland in the north of Scotland. The boy Thorfinn sat behind the knight (who had only taken to calling himself a knight after he had bought the patched nag from a horse dealer in Caithness – Sir James MacTavish was the knight's name).

Sir James wore a helmet and a breastplate, somewhat rusty, and he carried a pike, and in his belt an axe and a dagger. A bag of oatmeal and a little barrel of salted herring hung from the saddle.

Southward they rode, Sir James MacTavish and his squire Thorfinn out of Orkney. They had both been sick crossing the Pentland Firth on a fishing boat.

For miles and miles they met no one, then round a bend in the track they came on a man driving a few cows.

The man asked, very courteously, where they were bound for.

Sir James the knight said they were on their way to help the King of Scotland in his War of Independence against the King of England . . . The herdsman shook his head. Scotland? England? He had never heard of such places. All he knew was, he lived under Morven mountain and the Mackay was his chief and a hard man he was when it came to taxes. Oh yes, there was the great chief in the west, the Lord of the Isles. He had heard of a place further south called Alba. And there was a country over the sea, south-west, called Eire. But Scotland and England he had never heard of. Not once.

MacTavish and Thorfinn rode on. 'Ignorant peasant,' said MacTavish.

Sometimes they dismounted and ate a salt herring and a mouthful of ground oats. They drank, lying full-length on the bank, from swift-flowing streams. The knight had to remove his helmet to drink. His face was rough with sweat-stains and stubble.

'I hope we'll be there in time for the battle,' said Sir James MacTavish. 'We'll have to hurry.'

Thorfinn washed his face and hands in the river. Sir James clapped his helmet back on his head. The old horse Seamus groaned as knight and boy remounted. They turned his head southward.

They saw a spiral of smoke rising from behind a great rock.

'We'll buy a hot meal here,' said MacTavish. 'It's an inn.'

But when they rounded the great rock they came on a man sitting at the door of a rough stone house with a heather thatch. There was a heavy smell of malt, and three pots were bubbling and boiling over a fire and a large copper vessel stood on a tripod.

'Indeed,' said the man, 'I am making some whisky. And it is the water of paradise, or it will be in one year from now. And indeed, stranger with the iron mask, you and the boy would be most welcome to a cup of whisky, but look you, it is so new it would burn the throats out of you and drive you into madness. Come back in a year's time, you're most welcome, you'll think yourselves to be the grandest and happiest of mortals.'

They gave the whisky-maker a salt herring and a handful of oatmeal.

Slow golden bubbles broke on the surface of the three pots and enriched the wind.

'If you chance to meet the chief of Mackay's taxman on the road,' said the distiller, 'tell him Uisdean the barleyman is herding a flock on the far side of Morven. For if that scoundrel of a taxman knew I was making whisky in this secret place, he would be wanting to charge me for it, but the silver coin I gave him wouldn't be leaving his own pocket, the swindler.'

They left that little mountain distillery. The road led west. There, on the shore of a sea loch, they heard first the ringing of a small bell and then grave voices chanting. From time to time the solemnity turned to joy, the voices danced, an interweave of bass and treble, then after a pause the song seemed to be all awe and wonderment and praise.

They topped a rise and there was a little monastery above the loch shore.

The monks in the choir were singing.

Blessed be the Lord, the God of Israel, because he had visited and wrought redemption for his people . . . That, delivered from the hands of our enemies we should serve him without fear, in holiness and justice before him all our days . . .

'We won't get much to eat here,' said Sir James MacTavish to his squire. 'Depend on it.'

But when the monks' office was over and the monks trooped out of the chapel to attend to their beehives and their few sheep, the old prior greeted the travellers.

The knight told him they were riding to the wars, and they were hoping for a great sackful of spoils and (if they were extremely lucky) a captured English lord for whom they would get ransom money. Also, of course, they would establish Scotland's freedom for ever.

'Well,' said the prior, 'we know nothing here about such things. All our wars are against the principalities and powers of darkness. We are seeking the peace that is beyond human understanding. We are trying to unite our wills with the will of God – a difficult and a delightful thing to attempt, eight times a day in the choir, and in the solitude of our cells too of course. To work is to pray too – "laborare est orare" – and so we collaborate with the bees and the sheep and the herbs in praising God too.'

Just then the brothers – all of different ages, some toiling on a staff, others apple-cheeked (hardly older than Thorfinn) – drifted slowly towards the gate from fields around, and some came up from the fishing boat newly beached below, carrying fish.

'You will eat with us, travellers, before you fare south to your wars,' said the prior.

MacTavish and Thorfinn had their first hot meal, of grilled trout and new-fired bread, since they had left Orkney.

As they ate, a monk with hair and a beard so red it seemed his face was circled with fire, read aloud from a lectern. The text was in Latin, and so the knight and the squire couldn't follow it. 'It is the story of Magnus, the martyr of the northern isles,' said the prior, breaking a new loaf and sharing it with the Orkneymen. 'It is a very beautiful story.'

Sir James left a small bronze coin on the table when they left. Thorfinn thanked the monks, who stood in a smiling nodding circle all about him.

The prior bade them farewell at the monastery gate. 'May you come safely out of the fires of battle,' he said. He blessed them.

They rode on.

It was getting on for high summer, and every day brimmed with sunlight. They slept in goatskin blankets under the brief stars. They woke to lark-song.

The nag Seamus often stumbled and faltered. Then they rested by the roadside for a while. Sir James grumbled that they might be late for the battle, and that would be a shame on him forever.

As they were resting at a roadside, they heard a hulla-baloo and a snatch of song and a sudden fierce argument and a rattling of cans. Round the corner of the road came a tribe of tinkers, driving three donkeys laden with pots and pans, but the leading donkey was bestridden by a young man in splendid coloured rags from head to knee. Their feet were bare. On they rode, the tinkers, and the king of the tinkers gave from his donkey a loud greeting to Sir James and his squire.

The knight gave them no sign of recognition. But Thorfinn waved his hand to them.

On the tinkers rode, clanking and arguing.

But three young tinker men lingered behind the others. They stood on the road. They wondered, aloud, how much they might get in Inverness for the travellers' horse, and how much for the bucket on the head of the fat travel-ler; and they considered if there might be money in the knight's pouch, and whether the knight would be willing to loan them some to relieve their poverty, or whether it might not be necessary to persuade the knight.

Thorfinn's heart fluttered like a bird inside him.

Sir James MacTavish gave a roar of rage and got to his feet and swung his axe.

The three young tinkers laughed, as if this was the greatest of fun, then they turned and ran – laughing louder still – to join their company, disappearing now round a bend of the road northwards.

'It's a good job,' panted the knight, 'that I sharpened this axe before I left Norday . . .'

Faint and far-off came on the wind the echoes of the tinkers' mockery, their quarrelling and songs.

Knight and squire and nag were among mountain passes, high, when the weather changed and there was a day and a night of rain and wind. Indeed, one morning, when they crawled stiff out of their goatskins, there was a flurry of snowflakes.

Sir James was very bad-tempered that day. Thorfinn wished he was sitting warming his toes at the fire of Ingle in Orkney.

They prodded the horse to his feet, but Seamus seemed reluctant to move with those half-dozen snowflakes in his eyelashes.

'A stupid brute!' said Sir James MacTavish. 'Why did I ever buy the useless creature in Dunnett? Between a thick-headed nag and an idle stupid boy, I have some life of it, here on my way to help King Robert and Scotland . . .'

Then he gave Seamus a thwack on the flank with a piece of rope. Seamus turned on MacTavish with a fierce whinny, showing the strong teeth behind his black curling lip, and drove his hooves deeper into the mud.

Thorfinn whispered in the horse's ear, 'Come Seamus, time to be moving.'

And then Seamus allowed himself to be mounted and spurred on.

It was a frightening place they were in now, with a blue-gray chasm on one side of them and riven clefts of snow sloping steeply up on the other side. It was a sheep track they were on. At one place, a mile or so on, the path divided, one branch going up among the snows and the purple loaded clouds, the other descending into a pinewood.

Seamus the horse turned his head towards the trees. Sir James reined the horse round the other way. 'It's over the snow first, then down into the sun-bright plain,' he said.

Thorfinn thought the horse's instinct was more to be trusted than the knight's omniscience, but he knew better than to say anything, and so they took the slippery path upwards.

Gleams of sunlight drifted here and there about the mountains standing all round them. Once the clouds parted, and Thorfinn looked up to see an eagle circling high. Then the sky closed in and a cold cloud enwrapped them.

Seamus the horse plodded on gamely. Soon the narrow path petered out in a snowdrift. Seamus hesitated. 'Get on with you!' cried Sir James and dug the spurs in deep. Seamus and his riders faltered forward, slipped, stumbled, and soon all three creatures were lying struggling in thick snow.

Sir James thundered and threatened from his snow grave. Thorfinn wondered if their bones would ever be found. Even Seamus looked as if he would never see a blade of grass again.

'Well now,' said a voice near them, 'I have never in my

life seen horsemen so high up in this mountain pass. Would you be looking now for the road to Heaven? The way you're going you're not far from the crags.'

There beside them stood a shepherd with a sheep. He was carrying a young lamb over his shoulder.

'Come with me,' said the shepherd. 'I have a kind of a bothy not far from this place.'

Sir James and Thorfinn picked themselves out of the snowdrift and they followed the shepherd to the place where the paths forked, and there, further down hidden among the trees, was a log bothy.

The shepherd took a loaded skin bottle from a nail in the wall and passed it to Sir James, who took two quick gulps and then gasped as though a bull had butted him in the stomach. Thorfinn drank more cautiously, but his teeth and tonsils were wrapped in wild flame. A few seconds later, though, it seemed to him as though this shepherd's hut was better than any royal palace, and never in time had there been such an adventure as he was embarked on. Oh, it was indeed a most glorious thing to be alive, even though he was wet to the skin and his teeth were chattering!

The shepherd had lit a fine fire on his hearthstone and soon a pot of porridge was bubbling over the flames.

The shepherd's collie came and laid his head against Thorfinn's knee.

The shepherd took three horn spoons from hooks on the wall and bade them sup out of the pot. 'We don't have plates in a poor high place like this,' he said. 'You are most welcome. I have not seen one human person since I was in the church in Drumnadrochit at Easter.'

Thorfinn burned his mouth, supping the boiling porridge.

'Blow on it,' said the shepherd. 'Blow hard on the porridge with the sweet wind out of your youthful lungs, then the porridge will be a delight to you.'

The shepherd waited till the knight and the squire had eaten a few spoonfuls, then he crossed himself and put his own spoon into the pot.

Sir James, supping his porridge, washed it down from time to time with swigs of whisky from the bottle. Soon he began to say wild strange things. He said he thought it wasn't beyond him to take the English king prisoner – then with the immense ransom he'd buy up all the Orkney islands and the Shetland islands and Caithness, and the people there would be glad enough to have a famous wealthy warman such as himself, Sir James MacTavish, to be earl over them all . . . He said he would sail to royal courts and be on the best of terms with King Robert in Edinburgh, and King Edward in London might be glad to see his gallant captor from time to time. There was nothing to stop him sailing to see the Pope in Rome, either . . .

Sir James scraped the porridge pot with his spoon, with lip-smackings and mighty belchings. He had another deep draught out of the whisky-skin.

Then he said to the shepherd, 'You make passable whisky, my friend. I'm going to buy twenty carts and there'll be twelve barrels of your booze in each cart and we'll sell your whisky to every roadside inn in Scotland. I'll see to it that a butt of your famous gut-rot will be brought to King Robert's palace of Holyrood in Edinburgh, regularly once a month. King Robert and I are the best of friends – well, we will be, after the battle . . .'

Sir James's talk was now more mumbles than words. Suddenly the spoon clattered out of his hand and the great knight keeled over on the floor and went to sleep on the straw.

'No wonder he's tired after all that grand talk,' said the shepherd. 'What were the people called kings he was talking about? I've never heard a word or a title like that. And what are the places he spoke about, England and Scotland and Ireland and France? The only place I know is this mountain and the valley under it, and a clachan here and a sheep-cot there, and the grand village of Drumnadrochit. It is very sweet high language the horse-man speaks . . . Now, boy, I think you'd be none the worse of a little sleep yourself. My drink puts a fine drowsiness on a person; then when he wakes up it's the great new strength and eagerness he has for whatever lies ahead.'

Thorfinn didn't catch the last few words of the shepherd, for the thoughts in his mind blurred and his eyelids fell and folded like moths' wings, and when he woke up he was lying stretched out on the straw like his master.

Thorfinn felt quite blithe, getting to his feet. The shepherd was gone. Thorfinn could hear his voice lower down the mountain and the barking of the dog and a confusion of bleating. Sir James still snored on the floor – such powerful cataracts of noise poured from his throat, in pulses, Thorfinn wondered how the knight's skull wasn't fractured. He put his foot on Sir James's shoulder and pushed twice or thrice. Then the knight rolled over and groaned and rubbed his eyes and sat up.

'That shepherd,' he said, 'it's pure poison he distils here. The authorities will be told about this.'

Then he heaved brokenly to his feet and Thorfinn steadied him, and together they went out to where Seamus the horse was patiently grazing.

They mounted and rode carefully down the steep path.

At a turn of the road they passed the shepherd watering his sheep at a pool under a torrent.

'There you go now,' said the shepherd. 'You'll be sure to tell all the great and noble kings of the earth that Sorley the shepherd at Drumnadrochit was enquiring after them.'

The shepherd waved them a cheery farewell. Sir James gave a grunt, so ebbed-out he was with his hangover. But Thorfinn cried, 'Goodbye, Sorley the shepherd – goodbye, Bran the dog – goodbye, flock of sheep . . .' The boy's voice rang like a bell in the high mountain air.

On the road south, they were increasingly overtaken by troops of horsemen and in every little village they came to a group of young men who seemed to be saying farewell to mothers and wives and sweethearts, and some of the women were weeping and some were putting bread and cheese in the soldiers' knapsacks, and in one village an old woman was screeching if they didn't come home with victory they needn't come home at all. Then the young men in the villages shouldered their pikes and turned their faces to the south.

Sir James and Thorfinn, mounted on Seamus, passed solitary warmen burdened with claymores and small groups armed with axes and arrows. 'Saint Andrew and Scotland,' some of them called in passing. The knight, riding on, gave the ragbags of foot-soldiery cold greeting, but Thorfinn always pealed, 'Saint Andrew and Saint Magnus and King Robert'. (They had heard a rumour, before leaving Orkney, that some of the relics of Saint Magnus were to be carried south to the war.)

The town of Perth, once they had crossed the River Tay, was thronged with armed men. The inns were doing good trade, and the smithies rang with the fashioning of horseshoes and spear points. (Sir James MacTavish stopped to get a rivet fixed on his helmet – and Thorfinn wondered if it mightn't be a good idea to have Seamus new-shod, but Seamus struck the cobbles smartly with his hoof till they sent out showers of sparks.) At stalls all along the main street merchants were selling cheese, eggs, bread, whisky, smoked mutton and smoked fish, and they were charging high prices, but the sergeants and captains of the commissariat were buying ale and food in bulk, and throwing money about them like rain . . . Sir James grumbled about the expense. He bought a cheese as heavy and round as a curling-stone. 'This will have to do us till we get to the battlefield,' he said. It was goat cheese from the mountains westward: pungent wedges that almost stuck Thorfinn's jaws together.

Thorfinn had never seen such a busy place, nor such throngs of people, nor such haste and excitement at bargaining as in the town of Perth.

As Seamus trotted on south, strong from a nosebag of oats and sweet Tay water, Thorfinn fell asleep in the saddle, his head thudding gently against the fat shoulder of Sir James . . . They passed a wagon-train full of soldiers and weapons and provisions, but even the raillery of the soldiers failed to rouse the Orkney boy.

Thorfinn was wakened suddenly and violently. He found himself sprawled in a ditch. Nearby sat Sir James, struggling to get his helmet off his head, the metal still reverberating from its impact with the ground. Nearby Seamus limped and shivered and snatched an idle mouthful of

grass at the road verge. Something was wrong with
Seamus's left leg – he had stumbled and thrown them!

They might have to walk to the battle, like a couple of
ignorant camp-followers!

Sir James was feeling his right shoulder. 'This arm's all
numb,' Sir James complained. Thorfinn could see that it
was hanging loose.

'How can I fight in the battle now?' cried the knight.

Little groups of men were going past, southwards,
carrying pikes and clubs and rusty swords. They stopped
to look and laugh at Sir James, his beast and his boy.
Then they hurried on to Stirling Castle.

Thorfinn looked along the road that bore all this raggle-
taggle of troops. There, in the distance, dim against the
skyline, he could see Stirling Castle. The sun was just
going down behind it. The first star, a needle-point,
prinked the west, low down.

Then Thorfinn heard, from far in the south, the muffled
broken rhythm of a great army on the march. He set his
ear to the ground – there was no mistaking the tramp of
horses and men. Sir James heard nothing. He was too
busy holding his shoulder and moaning. It was hardly
audible, that onset. Thorfinn, his ear lost in wayside
flowers, could hear the slight trembling of the earth. Then,
faint and far off, he caught the thrill of a trumpet, which
was answered by another and another, lessening echoes
. . . It was the English army, marching to relieve the
castle.

Meantime the groups of men were streaming past more
urgently, and had no time to pause and make mockery of
the fallen heroes.

There was a great clatter of hooves on the road, a carriage jolted along with a troop of horse in front and

another troop behind. The rider in front carried a banner. 'Make way for the Earl of Mar,' he intoned. On they trotted. But soon the ordered hooves scattered to a halt, and the earl's carriage shuddered and was still.

The trouble was, Seamus had limped into the middle of the road and squatted down there, unable to go further. The horse looked at Thorfinn, his eyes full of pain and appeal. Thorfinn thought, 'You've done well, Seamus. The wonder is you've brought us as far as this.'

An old magnificent head with a russet and silver beard looked out from the carriage window. 'What's the matter now?' cried his lordship the Earl of Mar.

'Your honour,' said one of the outriders, 'an old nag has collapsed on the road and we can't get past.'

'Are you fools!' cried the earl. 'We've got to join the king. We're late as it is. A nag lame on the road – clear it out of the way. Be quick about it!'

'It isn't dead yet, your honour,' said the horseman.

'Am I cursed, that I have to live among dolts and imbeciles for ever! Get rid of it, now, at once.'

Six horsemen dismounted. One unsheathed his dagger and knelt beside Seamus.

Thorfinn closed his eyes.

There was a sudden thrash of hooves, the sound of a large body being trundled across the road and thrown into the ditch. Then the shaking of bridles, a cry from the leading horseman, 'On', and the lurch of the heavy carriage and the smart trot of the cavalry. A lantern had been lit inside the earl's carriage. A sergeant turned and said to the men in the rear, 'Let me remind you once more, men, your prime duty is to attack the English archers. They're the important ones. Cancel that iron sleet shower and the victory's half won. Those archers – the

French have lost their battles because of the English archers. Go for them at once! Trample them down.'

The horsemen responded with a shout.

In the fading light Thorfinn saw a vivid red splash in the middle of the road.

The light thickened. The sky was dark with rooks from the wood nearby. Those black birds would make a supper of Seamus's tongue and eyes and fresh unfestered wound. The crows wheeled and settled.

Thorfinn could not look.

He rolled himself in his blanket. He saw, before he closed his eyes, hundreds of campfires on the southern hillsides: the English host.

The base of Stirling Castle, miles away, was red with the Scottish campfires. A piper moved among the host, his music came thin and poignant and barbaric and proud on the wind.

Sir James stumbled about in the darkening field, muttering and mumbling to himself . . . The rooks cawed . . . A wolf howled nearby . . . Thinner came the keening of the bagpipes – the wind had shifted into the north.

Sleep, in a great purple wave, star-crammed, fell over Thorfinn.

When he woke, there was a great silence in the land. There was no sign of Sir James his master. Today was the day of the great battle. What did it mean, this silence? The reek of blood came on the wind. Wreaths and drifts of smoke clung about the castle rock.

'I must hurry,' said Thorfinn to himself. 'This must be the silence before battle. I must find Sir James MacTavish.'

Thorfinn had never known a silence like this. He

remembered the fowler Tammy Scott who had fallen over the crag. There lay the body of the fowler, broken between the reef and the rockpools. Half-a-dozen men stood about Tammy Scott. Thorfinn had a tight grip of his father's hand. The silence of that day was like this – only that had been a quiet country death, this silence was terrible and ominous and dangerous.

Thorfinn splashed his face in water in the burn – for a soldier should be clean, going into battle.

Along the road from the castle came a group of women. They were carrying a dead man on a straw pallet. The women walked quietly, but one of them – a girl – was weeping . . . Just behind them limped a soldier on a crutch, and another with a bandage round his head.

This means defeat, thought Thorfinn. He must have spoken the word aloud, because the oldest woman said, 'Victory? Defeat? What do they mean? We have lost the man who cut our corn and tended our sheep.'

Another of the group of women broke out into terrible lamentation. But the old woman bade her behave herself. 'Let the soul of the soldier go in peace. Say a prayer for him. Cease your howling.'

And the women went on, carrying their dead bread-winner.

Now the two wounded men came up with Thorfinn. 'Defeat,' said the soldier with the bandaged head. 'It was the most glorious victory ever won. God save King Robert. The English army – what's left of it – is trekking home over the Cheviot hills. Their king is riding to his ship at Dunbar.'

The other soldier said, 'I don't know whether my leg will mend or not. An arrow nicked me just above the knee. It's the most wonderful thing that ever happened to me, this wound.'

'Yes,' said his comrade, 'I don't care what happens to me now, from this day to the day of my death. Yesterday, at the Bannock Burn, we drank the cup of life to the full.'

The soldiers went on northwards, slowly. They laughed. The man with the wounded leg seemed to make a broken dance step or two.

They looked back at Thorfinn. 'You're too late, boy. It was the greatest day in the world. A pity for you . . .'

Then Thorfinn realized that he must have slept right through the battle.

A troop of ragged people crossed the hillside – all twelve of them were burdened with tent-poles, blankets, roasted haunches, coats and shoes, helmets and broken spears, spurs, saddles. Furtively they went, bearing the battle-spoils.

Thorfinn looked towards the commotion in the ditch. The rooks and rats and a wolf had almost reduced Seamus the horse to a jagged skeleton . . . Then Thorfinn touched salt at the corner of his mouth; he hadn't known he was crying.

The smart clip-clop of many horses, the creak of wheels, and round the corner came the Earl of Mar and his cavalry. Only now they had more horses, burdened – it must be – with battle-spoils. The horsemen looked like celebrants who, the day before, had feasted too well – they were gray in the face now and heavy-eyed. Inside the carriage the earl was deep in conversation with a golden-haired young stranger. In fact they were pledging each other in cups of red wine. With the lurching of the wheels, some of the wine splashed the white hand of the youth.

42

'Are you still here, boy?' said one of the corps to
Thorfinn. 'Well, it was a great day. Do you see that young
fellow sitting in the carriage with his lordship? That's the
Earl of Penzance. He's a prisoner. His lordship will get
ten thousand crowns for sending him home safe and sound
to his daddy and his mammy. No wonder his lordship's
treating the young fop to the best of meat and drink. It
would be terrible if the lad was carried off by measles or
the smallpox before the ransom was paid.'

The trooper took out his pouch and threw a coin to
Thorfinn. 'There you are boy,' he said. 'English gold. You
don't deserve it, dawdling here on the road. You'll be
late for your own funeral.'

Thorfinn picked the coin up. It was a silver groat, not
gold at all. (Soldiers get carried away in the exuberance
of victory.)

He ran after the cavalry. 'Tell me,' said Thorfinn, 'did
you see a knight called Sir James MacTavish in the battle?
I'm his squire.'

The horseman shook his head. The troop moved on.
Suddenly they began to sing, first one, then the whole
company.

> O freedom is a noble thing,
> Freedom makes men to have lyking . . .

On and round the bend of the highway they rode, singing
full-throatedly. In the silence between two verses Thorfinn
heard the mingled laughter of the two noblemen, deep bass
with mellow treble, the captor and the captive, and the tiny
clash as the rims of the silver winecups touched.

Another flock of plunderers crossed the hillside, even
more burdened than the first lot.

A black crow poked his beak into the eye holes of the horse's skull.

It struck Thorfinn that the main body of the Scottish army must be in pursuit of the enemy. That was why this country road had only a scattering of scavengers and the wounded.

He thought of Norday, and he had never felt so wretched and homesick and alone.

He heard soon the chime of a very small bell. A monk was walking along the road. The monk stopped when he saw Thorfinn. 'Bless you, boy,' he said. 'Have many wounded men gone this way?'

Thorfinn said there had been a few.

'The way it is,' said the monk, 'a few of them lie down and die at the roadside. I want if I can to give them viaticum and the last oil.'

Thorfinn asked the monk if he had seen a knight called Sir James MacTavish anywhere near the battlefield, alive or dead.

The monk shook his head. 'Hundreds have been killed,' he said. 'And still many are dying of their wounds. I must hurry on.'

'Is the castle captured?' said Thorfinn.

'King Robert has accepted the surrender of the castle from Sir Philip Mowbray,' said the monk. 'So I've heard. The king hasn't taken possession of the castle yet. That will happen sometime today. When King Robert stands at the great port of the castle, the bell will be rung thrice. Then all of Scotland will know of the outcome. There'll be dancing in the streets of Edinburgh and Perth and Aberdeen.'

The monk shook his head. There was a small tinkle somewhere inside the wide sleeve of his habit.

'With this bell,' he said, 'I go to look for the dying and the dead. May they rest in peace. Now bless you, boy. You're too young to be on this road of blood.'

Rats were scrithing among the ribs of Seamus the horse.

Then the monk and the boy heard it, a mighty threefold bronze trembling from the towered city. King Robert the Bruce was announcing victory to the world.

Thorfinn woke up in the smithy, his head against his father's shoulder.

The blacksmith had just finished shoeing Willum Holm's Clydesdale horse. The steel shoe was still trembling on the lifted forehoof of the patient beast.

Thorfinn looked round the faces of the village parliament. They rather resented having to postpone their debate until such time as Willum Holm's old horse had been clamorously shod . . . There was no sign of MacTavish.

'That'll be half-a-crown,' said Jock Seatter to Willum Holm.

'That MacTavish!' said Ben Hoy the sailor. 'What a blowhard! I swear I can't stand the man or his talk. If it wasn't that he keeps middling good ale, I'd never darken his door.'

The heat of the forge had made the men thirsty, and also the mention of MacTavish's good beer. One by one they levered themselves off the bench, and felt deep in their pockets to see if they had the price of a dram and a schooner.

Matthew Ragnarson lifted Thorfinn off the bench.

'We're going too,' he said, 'but not to the pub. You have your lessons to do and your mug of cocoa to drink. Then bed.'

45

Thorfinn was glad to know that MacTavish was still alive.

Before he left with his father he went up to Troy, the new-shod plough-horse, and stroked his neck.

'I can't take this brute to the pub, more's the pity,' said Willum Holm. 'And we both need a drop of ale, Jock, don't we, after our warstle with old Troy.'

When Thorfinn and his father neared home, there at the planticru wall stood Tina Lyde with a pot of rhubarb jam and a cherry cake for the table at Ingle. Matthew Ragnarson lingered to talk to her.

Thorfinn passed the woman without a word. Why was everyone in Norday saying that Tina Lyde was after their father and wanting to marry him?

At the table inside sat his sisters Inga and Sigrid and Ragna, playing ludo.

'You lazy idle useless boy,' cried Inga, 'it's too late to do your history lesson now. It's bedtime.'

Sigrid put on the milk to simmer for Thorfinn's supper.

A Man's Life

THE RAGNARSONS WENT to the island church every Sunday morning – Matthew Ragnarson walking in front, then the three sisters, all clasping their little bibles, and usually a good way behind, Thorfinn, looking at a butterfly or a stalk of grass.

Once inside the kirk, and having nodded to the two elders standing at the collection plate, the Ragnarsons mounted the stairs and sat in their usual gallery seat.

Most of the islanders went to church on Sunday morning, except for a few agnostics, atheists, and advanced thinkers (like Ben Hoy the ex-sailor and MacTavish the innkeeper and Mr Simon the schoolmaster).

The minister was Reverend Hector Drummond, a young man from the Borders. He was thought to be a passable preacher by the island men, though he lacked somewhat the fire-and-brimstone style of his predecessors. Yet all agreed that, reading the two scripture passages especially, the minister had a beautiful voice.

Reverend Hector Drummond's voice was so mellifluous

that Thorfinn Ragnarson was entranced from time to time. But the sermon lasted twenty-five minutes or half an hour, and then the boy often nodded off to sleep, until he was nudged awake by one of his sisters. The only thing that could guarantee Thorfinn's wakefulness during sermon-time was the passing round of the paper bag of sweets – pastilles or butternuts or cream caramels – every ten minutes or so.

One Sunday morning Thorfinn was moved, in spite of himself, by the Old Testament reading.

What profit hath he that worketh in that wherein he laboureth? I have seen the travail, which God hath given to the sons of men to be exercised in it. He hath made every thing beautiful in his time: also he hath set the world in their heart, so that no man can find out the work that God maketh from the beginning to the end. I know that there is no good in them but for a man to rejoice, and to do good in his life. And also that every man should eat and drink, and enjoy the good of all his labour, it is the gift of God. I know that, whatsoever God doeth, it shall be for ever: nothing can be put to it, nor any thing taken from it: and God doeth it, that men should fear before him. That which hath been is now; and that which is to be hath already been; and God requireth that which is past.

But the fine passage didn't prevent Thorfinn from dropping off half-way through the sermon, till he was jolted into wakefulness by a stern dig in the ribs from Sigrid his sister.

But immediately Inga consoled him with a butternut from the rustling poke of sweeties.

48

As they were leaving the church, everybody seemed to be whispering about a death.

'Yes, suddenly,' said Amos Smith the fisherman to Thorfinn's father Matthew. 'There we were getting the boats ready for sea on Saturday morning, when old Jacob keeled over among the stones and the seaweed, right beside his boat *Scallop*, and when we got to him he was gone. He went out like a light, Matthew. In half an hour he was cold as the shells . . .'

'I'll hurry on home,' said Ragna, 'and put the tatties on.'

Old Jacob Olafson was dead.

He had died on Saturday, the first fine day of April, with daffodils tossing their gold against the wall of Smylder, the Olafson croft.

Jacob had been taking a pinch of strong snuff out of his ebony snuff box between spells of working on his fishing boat *Scallop* down at the noust when it clattered out of his hand on to the rocks.

There he lay in the April sun, growing cold as the stones and the shells, until Dr Lamond arrived, bent over him, and shook his head.

And he had never attended the doctor in his life. Not once.

The news went all over Norday island quicker than the wind, that Jacob Olafson was dead. Those who hadn't heard, heard the next morning after the service.

Most of the islanders were sorry. A few were indifferent. One old woman on the far side of the island wiped her eyes on her apron. She had been Jacob's sweetheart one summer seventy years before.

Thorfinn Ragnarson had to pass the kirkyard on his way home from school, on the Monday.

49

There he saw Geordie Wylie the gravedigger busy with his bright spade, making a rectangular opening among the tombstones – some of the stones were new glittering granite, with names and inscriptions graven in goldleaf.

This was old Jacob Olafson's grave, half dug already. So Geordie Wylie informed the boy, pausing to lean on his spade.

Thorfinn Ragnarson wasn't sad. He had neither liked nor disliked Jacob Olafson. Jacob had just been there always, like the reef in the Sound, like the rock on the hill.

The thought that this old man was not part of the island any more, though – that filled the boy with wonderment.

Once, two years ago, Thorfinn had run past the croft of Smylder, eager to get down to the beach, for he had seen his father's lobster boat rounding the Gray Head, and, as he ran on, Smylder's flock of hens had risen in a red outraged flurry about his feet. Then old Jacob had shouted at him, and brandished his steel-tipped staff, and seemed to dance with rage, and that had frightened Thorfinn. He had thought, 'What a wicked old man!'

On the following Saturday, Isa Estquoy the shopkeeper had summoned Thorfinn who happened to be playing hop-scotch on the pavement outside, 'You, boy, take this basket of groceries up to Smylder, will you? Janet's in bed with the jaundice, old Jacob needs his bread and jam and *Sunday Post* and snuff. There's a fine chap.'

So Thorfinn, licking the lollipop that Isa Estquoy had given him, went happily most of the way, but more cautiously the nearer he got to the croft. He would set down the basket on the doorstep and knock and run away – anything rather than meet that wicked old man! Besides the other groceries, Thorfinn could see that there was a bottle wrapped in many sheets of newspaper – it could only be rum.

Jacob must have been on the lookout, from behind the curtain, for Thorfinn had no sooner set the basket on the doorstep than the door opened suddenly, and there old Jacob stood, all smiles. 'Weel done, boy,' he whispered, 'weel done. Thu're a clever boy, right enough. Yes, Janet's as yellow as a buttercup with the jaundice. But she'll be better soon. The hoose is fine and quiet. Either Janet sleeps or she moans like a doo. I can sit in peace withoot being ordered here and there – *Wash your face! Don't spit tobacco juice in the hearth! It's good porridge – it does NOT have lumps in it. Shift till I sweep the hearth.* . . Thu're a smart lad, thu'll go far. What's thee name? Oh, Matthew Ragnarson's boy . . . Let me see, is me medicine in the basket? Oh yes, it is. Janet would never put this kind of tonic on the shopping list – never! But it's kept me healthy for eighty years. So I just wrote "one bottle Old Barbados rum" with a blunt pencil at the end of the list Janet whispered to me from her bed . . . Never never mention this rum to anybody, boy, it's none of their business anyway. This island's full of inquisitiveness and gossip. I used to have a dram every night when me wife was alive, after work, and that kept me gaan through winter snows and harvest sweats. But when Janet grew up and took charge o' things, I wasna allowed the smell o' a cork . . . Thu'll go far, boy, I can tell that. Here, tak this.'

And the old man dug deep in his trouser pocket and dredged up a shilling, and put it in Thorfinn's rapturous palm. A shilling was a fortune! (He got a penny on Saturday from his father.)

And all the while Thorfinn could hear Janet's plaintive

51

voice from inside, 'Who's that at the door? What are you being so secret about? Oh, I don't trust you, daddo . . . Have you fed the hens? Oh, why do I have to get jaundice just when it's hatching time and daffodil time!'

The old man patted the departing boy on the head.

That was the last time Thorfinn ever had dealings with Jacob Olafson.

And tomorrow Jacob was going to be put into that black hole, in a box shaped like a boat, and he would never be seen again by mortal eyes.

Thorfinn sat on the kirkyard wall in the spring sunlight and thought about birth and life and death.

'*A thousand ages in thy sight/Are as an evening gone . . .*' They had sung that hymn in the kirk on Sunday.

It was very true. The life of a man, thought Thorfinn, is a brief voyage, with the ocean of eternity, the many-voiced sea, all around.

Thorfinn drowsed sitting there on the kirkyard wall. Through his dream, from time to time, he heard the bright chime of the gravedigger's spade on stone.

*   *   *

See, there he is, the new-born child, in his little ship of time, his cradle.

It is early morning – sunrise – the ship and solitary voyager have been cast on to this island, out of the vast of eternity. A young mother bends and kisses the stranger. The young bearded father lifts him into the light.

The child, little Jacob Olafson, cries. Is it grief for the marvellous country he has left? Every child weeps at birth, as if he knew the sorrows that he must meet on his voyage.

Yet the free spirit must have been willing to undertake the journey . . .

The sun takes one golden step up the east. A boy is running and laughing among the sheep on his father's hill. The dog barks beside him. Today the flock must be rounded up for the annual sheep-dipping. His father calls from the barn below, 'Don't frighten the ewes, Jacob!' . . . The boy's sister is calling to Peg the cow – it is milking time.

There, on the beach below, the boy Jacob Olafson can see Angus the beachcomber moving about in the big ebb, seeing what he can find after the westerly storm at the weekend . . .

The sun takes another golden step up the sky.

It is breakfast time in Smylder.

A few years have passed. It is also Jacob's last day at school.

'Well,' said Jacob's mother, 'you'll be a great help to your dad from now on. The farm work hasna been easy for him since the rheumatics got into him. Thank the Best, you're a strong healthy lad.'

Jacob sulks.

Jacob puts his horn spoon back into his bowl of half-supped porridge. Jacob mutters that he has promised to help his uncle Archie at the fishing all summer in Archie's boat *Scallop*. (Archie is his mother's oldest brother, a bachelor.) Besides, he mumbles, why can't his golden-haired sister Madeline help on the farm? She's big and strong. She loves that kind of work, Madeline. Next winter she'll be fourteen and finished with school.

'This peedie croft's been worked for three hundred years by Olafson men,' says his mother sharply. 'And you'll go on working it, you and your bairns after you.'

Jacob kicks the table leg till the porridge bowls dance on the table top.

Madeline laughs and goes out to feed the hens.

'Noo, Jacob,' says his mother gently, 'your dad has a lobster boat too, the *Susanna*. . . You'll be a great help on board the *Susanna*, I'm sure, when it's idle days on the farm. Go oot noo and help your dad to single the neeps – he finds his shoulders very sore when he has to stoop.'

The boy sups the rest of his porridge and goes out into the bright windy day.

There's his father with his hoe in the turnip field, and Madeline is crossing the field with a hoe to help him, after milking the cow Peg.

Jacob looks seaward.

Archie his uncle is on the beach below, stowing lobster creels into the *Scallop*. As soon as the tide turns, Archie Sabiston will turn the *Scallop* towards the western crags, where underseas the lobsters are moving this way and that on the ocean floor like knights in blue armour.

Jacob runs shouting through the fields to the boat noust. 'Archie, wait for me! I'm coming with you.'

His father and sister go on working in the field.

His mother looks at him from the open sun-smitten door, shading her eyes . . .

So quickly it passes, the little day of a man's life on earth.

The sun has climbed higher towards the zenith, another golden step.

There is great excitement at Smylder.

In a week's time there's to be a marriage in the little barn: Madeline to Jock Seatter the young blacksmith.

Great preparations are in train. Millie Smith the seamstress is making the bride's dress. All the neighbouring women have been baking and brewing, and making plans for the biggest wedding feast Smylder has known for a century past; for Madeline is the first daughter in the croft to be married for three generations.

Jock Seatter, the bridegroom, has ridden on his bicycle with verbal invitations to a score of crofts and farms and village houses. This is Jock's third night of 'bidding'. At every house he has gotten whisky and ale. One night he is long in getting back to the smithy. Madeline goes looking for him. She finds him sleeping in a ditch underneath his bicycle. 'Little use talking to a drunk man,' says Madeline. But next morning Jock the blacksmith gets, for the first time, the sharp edge of her tongue . . .

The minister, old Mr Snoddie, has been notified. The marriage will take place in the Manse. There will be a wedding procession, with a fiddler, to the Manse, then back again to the barn of Smylder.

'Jacob, you're to be the groomsman. I'll let down the hems of your Sunday suit. You're growing still, though you're 20. The wedding ring, you must have the keeping of that. Be sure and have it safe in your waistcoat pocket . . .' So his mother has instructed Jacob.

Now poor Will Olafson, the crofter of Smylder, can hardly move with rheumatism – 'arthritis' is the new name the doctor gives it. He is like an animal in a trap – every movement is an agony for him . . . But he is putting a brave face on it – he'll be there at his daughter's wedding, to give her away to her husband.

The day has come. The trestle tables are brought into the barn. In a half-dozen crofts round about, hens are burbling in soup pots, and home-cured hams are sliced, and bannocks are taken from the blue reek of griddles.

Madeline, in front of the long mirror, looks like a snow princess.

'Jacob, we've found a tartan tie to wear with your new white shirt. Come and try them on . . .'

But there is no sign of Jacob, the groomsman.

Ah, he must have wandered up to the hill, or down to the shore – anywhere to be away from the incessant babble of the wedding women in Smylder.

But Jacob is still not home at dinnertime. His broth grows cold on the table.

The young woman from the next croft, Toft – Mrs Olafson fondly hopes that some day Bertha Swanson of Toft might be Jacob's bride, such a good-hearted hard-working lass she is – is sent out to look for Jacob and summon him home for the fitting of the groomsman's suit.

Bertha comes back in an hour. She has searched Norday island high and low. She has walked across the peat hill and along the shore, and even put her face into the inn, but there was no sight or sign of Jacob.

The women look up from their carving of meat and fowls, and their stirring of broth-pot and clattering of plates, and there is silence in Smylder for a full minute.

His mother is white in the face.

'Ah well,' says Will Olafson, from his chair of pain. 'What will be, will be.'

It was a maimed wedding, as things turned out. For Jacob didn't come home in time for the wedding, neither to Smylder to put his best suit on, nor to carry the gold ring in his waistcoat pocket to the ceremony at the Manse, nor to dance and drink the bride's cog at the feast in the barn.

It had hurriedly to be arranged for Jacob's cousin Tommy Amund to act as groomsman. And of course – Tommy being a stout thickset youth – he filled Jacob's wedding suit to bursting – and he put the ring in the wrong pocket, so that the ceremony in the Manse was held up for a couple of fumbling flustered minutes.

The bride Madeline looked anything but happy, and Mrs Olafson sat throughout with her head in her hands, and from time to time her shoulders shook. (It is not done, to show your emotions too grossly.)

And Will Olafson stood crookedly on two sticks, after handing over his daughter to her man, and hid his pain.

Jacob Olafson didn't come back that night, or any day that week. Month followed month – there was no word of him.

The police office in Kirkwall was notified. A search was made under the cliff, and in the loch, and in the three quarries. There was no sign of Jacob, alive or dead.

At the beginning of winter, Jess the tinker wife arrived with her pack of trinkets and needles and cotton drapery in Norday, and drifted from house to house, making a small sale here and getting cheese and a mug of ale there. At last Jess set down her pack beside the fire at Smylder.

'Ah,' said Jess, 'I don't think I'll be coming this way again. I've gotten gey weary, this past summer, trudging through Orkney and Shetland and Caithness with this pack. It gets heavier by the week.'

Mrs Olafson brought her a cup of tea and a piece of currant loaf.

'Where,' said Jess, 'is the bonny lass of this house?'

She was told Madeline had been married a year and had a young child in the smithy-house, a pretty daughter called Anna-Mary.

Jess the tinker wife looked at Will Olafson, where he sat crooked and gray in the face in his strawback chair.

'You and me, mister,' said Jess, 'I think we'll be meeting soon in a better place . . .' And she sighed once or twice over her broken cake.

Will Olafson said nothing but looked into the ashes of the hearth.

'Don't ask about Jacob our son,' said Mrs Olafson. 'He's vanished clean off the face o' the earth. In the aald days it would have been said, *the trows had taen him*. I don't think we'll ever set eyes on Jacob again.'

'I think neither you nor your man will ever set eyes on him again in this life,' said Jess. 'But he'll come back to Smylder for sure. Didn't I see him with my own eyes stepping on board that Hudson's Bay ship the *Windward*, in Hamnavoe harbour, the very day he was supposed to be standing in front of the minister passing the golden ring to the bridegroom . . . ? I warrant you, he'll be home again, once he has a bag of sovereigns sewn in his sark. Who could bide long in them wastes of snow and ice, wolves and walruses, Eskimos and Indians! . . . Never think of selling Smylder, mistress, the son and heir will be home some day, I warrant you.'

Mrs Olafson gave a cry of joy, but quieted soon, for it is not a done thing to show your emotions openly in Orkney.

She looked at her goodman Will, sitting there in his strawback with tear-glitterings in his beard.

Such a short day is the life of man – brief labour and love and laughter between dawn light and the first star in the west. Round Norday island, the great ocean music goes on and on, everlastingly.

But this life – if Jacob Olafson is still alive – is not long past its meridian.

The sun has reached the zenith of noon, and has taken two golden steps down the west: if all is well with the vagrant. If not . . .

One morning a bearded man and a black-haired dark-complexioned hawk-nosed woman step off the ferry boat at Norday pier. The man has a box with a padlock on his shoulder.

The young ferryman Andrew Rosey asks the strangers if he can direct them anywhere, after he has gotten his fare money.

The man shakes his head. The woman looks confused and frightened.

A few island men are standing at the pier; there they always gather when the ferryboat comes in. (It is five years yet before the steamer service starts.)

Without appearing to be inquisitive, the islanders put occasional sidelong probing looks on the strangers as they walk side by side up the pier and into the village inn.

Old Eddie Moss says, 'That's a face I ken, but I can't put a name to it. The woman's an Indian from the Canadian nor-wast, no doubt aboot that. What noo?'

The man and the squaw take the road that goes west out of the village, and they do not stop till they reach the croft of Smylder.

The man puts down his sea-chest and sits on it. The squaw lingers at the wall of the cabbage patch, or planticru.

There is no welcome for them – that much is sure: no barking dog, no flutter of hens, no smoke from the chimney. One window is shuttered, the other has a broken pane. The door looks withered, the roof stands badly in need of re-thatching. The remnant of the peatstack has all but mouldered into brown dust.

The man sits for a while on his sea-chest.

Then he gets to his feet suddenly and lets fly a violent kick at the door. The lock is so rusted, the door flies open at once.

And then the man and the woman go into the cold spider-and-mouse-infested croft.

When Mrs Madeline Seatter comes later that morning, after she has heard in the smithy-house that strangers have broken into her dead parents' house Smylder, she sees smoke coming from the chimney. The house breakers, having no heat, have lit a fire in the stove by smashing up the decayed hen-house. Her mother's kettle is singing and snorting on the stove. The man and the Indian woman are sitting on each side of the stove sipping hot grog.

'Weel Jacob,' says Madeline, 'thu took thee time getting home for the wedding. That was ten years ago. But I'm blyde to see thee, boy.'

Orkney folk didn't kiss in public in those days, but the brother and sister put shy joyful looks on one another.

'This is Rena, my wife,' says Jacob. 'Be easy with the lass, Madeline. She's frightened in this strange place.'

'You can't bide here with Smylder in a state like this,' says Madeline. 'There's a room to spare in the smithy-house. It'll be a bit noisy, with the anvil ringing and two young bairns laughing and greeting from morn to night. There's plenty of meat and fish and bread and cheese and ale.'

60

Jacob thanks his sister, but says he'll pay for their lodging until such time as he and his Labrador wife can move into Smylder permanently.

'Thee father'll rest quiet in his grave,' says Madeline. 'His field'll be ploughed, and the hill grazed. Our mother too – she died two years ago – she'd be blyde to ken Rena will be lighting the fires and bringing in water from the well . . . Another winter, and Smylder would have been a ruckle o' stones.'

Jacob says he'll see, after a month or so, what is what. Maybe Rena will sicken for the snow, the wide rivers of beaver and sturgeon, the black immense forests – in that case, he'll have to take her home. And Jacob isn't all that sure about ploughing and harvesting. He has always liked fishing best, the things of the sea. He might sign on a cargo ship, sailing out of Hamnavoe to Singapore or Boston and come back every couple of months or so with some money. For, as things are, he's poorer now than when he ran away from Orkney ten years before.

In the smithy, an hour later, Jock Seatter greets them gravely. Oh yes, to be sure, they can bide at the smithy-house till the half-ruined croft is put in some kind of order. He goes so far, the good blacksmith, as to take Rena by the hand and offer her the only seat in the smithy, a wooden stool with a leather cushion on it.

And now the two young Seatters – a boy and a girl – come in shyly to see the uncle they have heard about (not always kindly, after his desertion on the wedding day) but never seen. And they gaze out of great blue eyes at the dark-skinned Indian woman with the long straight black hair and nose curved like a hawk.

Presently Madeline comes from the kitchen to say that

dinner is on the table, broth and boiled haddock and tatties.

Jacob works hard up at Smylder to make it habitable.

Jock Seatter lends him fifty pounds to buy a few sheep and a milking cow and a little flock of hens.

Neighbours come from the crofts with sacks of peat to make a fire, until such time as Jacob and Rena can cut peat on their own hill-banks in May.

The woman is shy. She moves into an out-house like a shadow if she sees a neighbour coming to speak to Jacob about this or that business, and only emerges when the neighbour has gone away again. Often that takes some time, for the visiting crofter or fisherman wants to know all about the nor-wast, the whaling in Davis Straits and the Hudson's Bay fur-trading, and Jacob tells his stories in a slow cautious way. (The same ten or twelve stories, as the years pass, become ever more colourful and dramatic, so that it is hard in the end to recognize them from the bare original narratives; but the story-teller and his listeners are all the more pleased because of that.)

The rusted plough in the barn has a sack of seed-corn lying humped beside it against the wall, ready for spring. The roof has a new thatch. A young collie barks from the end of the house at everyone passing. The breaches in the hill-dyke are mended. Two new windows glitter on the front of Smylder. In barn and byre and stable, a thousand cobwebs are swept aside as if by a great gale. Jacob has a will to work, no doubt about that.

A half-grown kitten sits on the doorstep, eyeing the starlings and the voles with bright-eyed curiosity.

The last snow melts from the summit of the hill.

Jacob, until he can afford to buy a plough horse, gets

the loan of an aged but strong ox to plough out tilth that has been idle now for ten years and more.

One day, when Jacob drags wearily back from the half-ploughed field, Rena is there at the end of the house to meet him.

For months she has been a shy furtive fugitive creature, half afraid of everyone and everything. Once or twice Jacob has thought, 'This can't go on. She'll sicken and die in this green island. I think I'll have to take her back to Baffin Bay. And if I do go back with her, will I ever return to Orkney?'

Only occasionally has a cry of something like joy rung out from her mouth, two weeks before when Jenny the new cow was led home by Jacob . . . And again when she discovered a starling's nest in the eave with a cluster of eggs in it – and then, next morning, when she went to look again, the new-hatched chicks. Then her lips had parted, and her black eyes melted with delight.

But mostly, it was the look of far melancholy.

Today she says, 'I like it here, man. I will stay.'

After that, it is no time at all before she can bake bannocks, and spin and knit, and see to the water and the never-dying fire on the hearth, almost as well as any other Norday woman.

And she goes to the village shop, and learns the value of merchandise against shillings and pence. She can exchange a few words with some inquisitive gossip on the way home.

She goes to the kirk piously every Sunday morning with her bible in her hand, gliding along beside her heavy-footed dark-coated husband.

And so Smylder is restored to life.

But not, alas, for long. A child is born, a child with a

few dark strands of hair and sloe-black eyes. The mother dies.

The harvest this year has been all cut, a fair bounty.

Jacob wanders down to the noust where his boat is, the *Scallop*. His uncle Archie left it to him three years before.

He sits and looks out over the sea till the first star glitters in the Atlantic.

From that day on – though he doesn't neglect the farm work entirely – he spends most of his life in the fishing-boat. He often speaks about selling up and going for a sailor.

'Don't be a fool,' says Madeline severely. 'You have a bairn to provide for. She can bide at the smithy-house till she's twelve or fourteen, then back she goes to Smylder, to look after you. Besides, you still have a lot of debts to settle. Go to sea? What skipper do you think would ever sign on a clodhopper like you with the first gray hairs in your beard? You have a barnful of barley to thresh. See to that.'

But Jacob goes to the lobsters when all the other Norday men are busy with their farm work.

Jacob's field is the last to be ploughed. His barley is the last to be threshed. And this happens year after year.

Now the day of this man's life has its first onset of shadows. The sun is going down in the west, step after step. The island hollows and ditches begin to fill.

Jacob Olafson's beard is meshed with gray and silver.

He potters about between his barn and his fishing-boat *Scallop*. He gets adequate rewards for his labours, no more. He seems, after a day at the lobsters, to be more tranquil than after ploughing or tattie-howking. He is inclined to grumble, coming in from the fields. Janet his daughter has a hard time of it, trying to please him, laying out his snuff-box and jug of mulled ale beside the fire. It is as if the cattle and sheep, the oats and turnips, are conspiring with the stars in their courses against him. He rarely laughs or smiles.

Jacob is not the best-liked man in the island. 'An awkward body,' the younger wives say in the village shop or at the well.

And the children, passing Smylder on their way to school, keep well out of range of his thick staff.

Everyone says what a treasure that lass Janet is – what would Jacob Olafson do without his growing daughter with the dark eyes and the long straight black Cree hair?

As the years pass, Janet learns to stand up for herself. 'You look after the barn and the fishing-boat,' she says. 'I'm in charge here, at the hearth and the spinning-wheel and the butter-kirn . . . Don't spit tobacco juice on the hearth! Who's going to eat the scones I spread out there on the warm stone? . . . And I want to find no more rum bottles under the bed – yes, I'll smash them. I will, I'll scatter the last drop over the dunghill! . . .'

So, Jacob Olafson, growing old with rheumaticky winter pains in shoulder and haunch-bone, and slowly blurring sight, thinks it well to let his half-Indian daughter have her way inside the croft house.

He doesn't admit it, even to himself, but he has a dread that some young island man or other will come about Smylder, under the stars, to court her. Whatever would become of him if he were left alone?

So he speaks harshly to any young fellow who chances to linger round the planticru, or who speaks overlong to Janet at the grocery van on a Friday morning on the road outside.

But Janet seems not to be at all interested in suitors. She is quite happy with the cow, the flock of hens, the butter and cheese making, the baking and the brewing and spinning. The long gray wool flows from her fingers, taut and tough and fluent. Her white cheeses crumble at the first touch of the knife.

Even old Jacob acknowledges that Janet's broth is 'not bad' – by that he means that it is very good soup indeed. A tinker sits on the doorstep, among the first snowflakes, and drinks a mug of Janet's hot ale, and feels the glow in his toes and umbles and finger-ends.

Jacob comes in grousing from the lambing hill – everything has gone wrong – but after a plate of Janet's oatcakes spread thick with butter, he thinks things might come out all right in the end – the new lambs, though thirled to life on delicate threads, might live . . .

Old Jacob is happiest on a fishing day, when he unmoors the *Scallop* and sets out westward with haddock lines or lobster creels. Those mornings, he croaks and croons a whaling ballad before his porridge. Even before he leaves the house for the boat noust, there's a sparkle in his eyes like the sun on the sea. 'Smoked fish,' he says to Janet, 'get ready to smoke a basketful of haddocks and see that you smoke them a bit longer than you smoked them last time . . .'

Then there's no more talk of rheumatics in his shoulders. The old man turns his back on the hill and ploughland and sets out with a nautical swagger and lurch towards the seabirds, the *Scallop* and the waves.

The trouble is, on such days he's inclined to stop at the village inn before coming home to Smylder with his catch. Then it might be midnight before Janet, lying sleepless, hears 'My bonnie lies over the ocean', or 'Heave away, heave' coming on the wind, a raucous tipsy rant. And then the old man rattling the latch, but not getting in, for Janet has barred it from the inside. His roars of rage then until she comes and unbars the door! . . . She does it as softly and swiftly as a shadow, and is back in her bed before he comes blundering into the lobby, growling and threatening.

Tomorrow morning, at the breakfast table, it is Janet who will do the talking. Another carry-on like last night, and she'll walk out on him. She will. Two or three of the big farms would be glad of her services – time and again she's been approached, and she'd have more wages and less worries than in this rum-besotted hovel . . .

It is Jacob who runs away – one day, quite suddenly, when he's in Hamnavoe selling a few sheep at the mart there. He meets an Aberdeen trawler skipper in the 'Arctic Whaler', a Hamnavoe hostelry, and over tots of rum Jacob must have agreed to go on an Iceland fishing trip with him . . . It's three weeks before he climbs out of the rusty trawler on to the big pier of Hamnavoe, and walks twelve miles to the Norday ferry. He is gray in the face with ice-floes and sickness, bonded rum and the northern lights. Also the sea and the salt have sharpened the pains in his shoulders and legs; it is a long toilsome walk from the village pier and the inn, to Smylder.

'So you're back,' says Janet sweetly. 'I don't want to know where you've been. I got on well enough. In fact, I've enjoyed myself this past three weeks better than since I was a bairn. You should go away more often.'

But Jacob never signs on for a crewman again.

'Oh lass,' he says, 'you wouldna believe what they gave

me to eat on that trawler. The pigs at the trough fare better.'

The sun has only one russet clouded step to go now, then it will be under the horizon.

The day of his life will be over for another man born into this vale of tears.

Jacob Olafson died suddenly, working on the *Scallop* down at the beach, on a beautiful spring morning.

A few other fishermen were working nearby, painting their boats, mending their creels, holding up fingers now and then to test the wind.

Jacob Olafson was crooning a verse of 'Andrew Ross the Orkney sailor', when the ballad broke off and they heard a single cry. Then the eighty-year-old man fell beside the *Scallop*.

When the fishermen got to him, Jacob was dead, the light frozen in his eye.

When six of them brought the body up to Smylder, covered with a sail, Janet said, 'Ah, that was a good way for him to go.'

She found a bottle of his rum she had been hiding from him in the peat-stack, and she poured cups of grog for the fishermen. Gravely they pledged the quiet shape lying on the flagstone floor.

Then Janet asked Bill Halcro if he would make four visits – to the registrar, Albert Laird the joiner who made coffins as well as tables and doors, the minister, and Geordie Wylie the gravedigger.

*   *   *

Thorfinn was wakened from his dream by an extra loud clang of the gravedigger's spade on stone.

The dream cheered him, in a way – for him the day of life had hardly begun, the sun was just over the hill of Selskay island in the east.

He had much to do and to enjoy still, surely, while the light lasted.

'You, boy,' said the gravedigger, 'hadn't you better be off home for your tea? There's old Jacob's grave dug. Tomorrow's the funeral.'

Beside the earth opening, the new-dug grave, a mound of clay reared up like a wave.

The sun was down. The first star was trembling over the still Sound.

Thorfinn heard hammering inside Albert Laird's workshop in the village.

Albert was putting the finishing touches to a coffin, Jacob Olafson's death-ship.

Tomorrow the wave of clay would break over it.

At the end of his house Tina Lyde was standing with a basket on her arm. 'Is that you, Thorfinn?' she whispered. 'Have you had a good day at the school? I've just made some rhubarb jam and cheese. Here, you don't need to say who gives them.'

'We don't want charity,' said Thorfinn. 'My father and sisters and me, we manage fine without anybody's help. Just leave us alone.'

Inside the house, Matthew Ragnarson was lighting the paraffin lamp.

Broch

THORFINN RAGNARSON HAD often been puzzled by a circular ruin that stood on the edge of the shore – a mere waist-high ring of stone – half a mile from his father's croft.

Nobody in Norday was quite sure what the structure was. Matthew Ragnarson his father said it had been there all during his lifetime, exactly the same as it was today. It was marked on the old maps – it had always been there, unchanging.

But 'No,' said his father when they were out looking for a lost sheep one day, 'it was a bit higher, now I come to think of it, when I was a boy. The sea's washed some of it away, too. It isn't a complete circle now. When you're a grandfather, boy, there'll be nothing here at all maybe. This coast is eroding away so fast.'

Matthew Ragnarson had no idea what the structure might have been – a primitive mill, maybe, or a Celtic church, or an early lighthouse that the islanders had set up to keep ships from the rocks – on winter nights they'd have lit, maybe, a fire on the top . . . Thorfinn doubted the lighthouse theory. He had heard often enough how glad of a shipwreck the Norday men of two centuries ago and more had been, so hard were the lives of the country folk and the fishing folk in those times.

Even as he and his father watched, that day, a bigger wave came out of the sounding flood-tide, and washed against the truncated ruin, and another stone tottered on its base and fell into the swirl and seethe of water, and became one with the shore stones.

They heard a plaintiveness on the wind from further round the crag. There was the lost sheep, exiled on a ledge.

Maggie the old ewe *was* pleased to see them . . .

It was a fine Friday afternoon at the beginning of summer. There were only a few days to go before the start of the long holiday.

Mr Simon was in high good humour. He had just received by post a brochure about holiday-making in Brittany, and he was looking forward to going there with his lady-friend from Falkirk. Miss Cameron, also a school teacher, had visited Norday at Easter. 'She'll clip his wings, that one,' Bella Simpson and Tina Lyde and Isa Estquoy decided in the island shop. (Miss Cameron had just been shopping in the village, and she had been as bold as brass, feeling the oranges and onions to see if they were in good heart, and telling Isa Estquoy that nearly all the items in her shop were too dear, far too dear. 'In Falkirk, I can buy that same jam for a penny less. And that tin of beans on your shelf is a ha'penny too dear . . .'.)

'Well,' Isa Estquoy had said sweetly to her, in her tiny

voice, 'in that case, you're at perfect liberty to shop elsewhere . . .'

Whereupon the glowering dark-handsome Miss Cameron had retreated – there was no other shop in the island for her to go to.

'She should have been a prison-wardress, that one,' said Tina Lyde, 'not a school teacher.'

'She'd have made a good Viking, cracking skulls with a club,' said Bella Simpson. 'She should be a man, not a woman at all. The poor bairns in the school she teaches in!'

'If you ask me,' said Isa Estquoy, 'they're well matched, Mr Simon and Miss Cameron. They'll tear each other's hair out. They might even enjoy that.'

Albert Laird the joiner came in for an ounce of bogey roll. He smelled strongly both of tobacco and pine-wood shavings, from a cradle he was making.

The women rallied Albert Laird, with much laughter, asking him if the cradle was for a happy event sometime soon in his house. Albert and his wife Annie had been married and childless for forty years. But no, he said, it was a special order for Millie Smith the seamstress. (Millie Smith was seventy-five years old, and a widow since the age of twenty, when her man Thomas had been lost off the fishing boat *Lucky Lass*.)

The three women in the shop shrieked with mirth.

'When,' said Albert Laird, 'may I expect to have an order from one of you ladies for a fine new cradle of the best Oregon pine?'

The three were more convulsed with mirth than ever. 'Oh, Albert,' squealed Isa Estquoy, 'you'll be the death of me! . . .' The words sobered Isa Estquoy up a little, for it struck her all at once that Albert Laird also made

73

coffins; and Isa hadn't felt all that well this past spring: rheumatics and a cough.

'Here's your tobacco,' she said. 'That'll be elevenpence ha'penny.'

Just then the island's only person of quality came in: Mr Harcourt-Smithers the laird. Mr Harcourt-Smithers spent two summer months in Norday Hall. He wintered in London. He went to the Caribbean and the Pacific in spring and autumn on a luxury cruise-ship. Now he was an elderly widower who, it was said, had suffered a mild stroke. His two teenage granddaughters came to stay with him in the summer months.

At sight of Mr Harcourt-Smithers, the women put their laden baskets over their arms and left the shop. Mr Harcourt-Smithers was fat and red faced. He puffed and blustered and felt for his wallet. Albert Laird cut an end of bogey roll with his knife and rubbed it in the palms of his huge red hands, then filled his pipe. 'Morning,' said Mr Harcourt-Smithers in a kind of loud broken bark. Isa Estquoy squeaked a kind of greeting. The joiner grunted, and struck a match and left the shop, leaving a trail of reek in the air.

'Be so good,' said Mr Harcourt-Smithers. 'Send a couple bottles of Old Orkney whisky up to the Hall. Expecting the bishop from Aberdeen. Coming on the steamer *Raven* this afternoon. Be a choppy crossing, I think. Bishop an old man. Be cold. Be sick maybe. Need a toddy.'

Out in the bay the freshening blue wind was putting crests on the sea.

A wave in the Sound – one of those seventh waves that comes in higher and colder and more rampant than the six ordered predictable waves on either side of it – crashed against the round ancient ruin on the shore, and carried away another stone that had stood for twelve centuries. That stone would trundle here and there with the tides, flung back and fore in the mill of ocean for a few decades, growing smaller and ever more spherical, until it was at last a scattering of sand among the oyster grains and the grains of crab and cormorant.

A hundred years on, and a child might be building a sand castle on the edge of the tide, on a summer afternoon.

It was a few days before the summer holiday.

Mr Simon was giving the school a special treat. He was taking the flock of children round the ancient monuments of Norday – the single standing stone beside the loch, the stone-age burial chamber, the foundations of the little Celtic church on the off-shore tidal island.

Now here they were at the truncated circular tower that was being slowly eaten by the sea.

'This,' said Mr Simon, 'is a *broch*, all that's left of a primitive castle of two thousand years ago. Of course it was much higher when it was in its prime. And strong, it was almost impregnable. (Willie Vass, what does the word "impregnable" mean? . . . You stupid boy . . .) If we look closely, we can see that the broch was bonded with a double wall, between which a spiral stair wound up for forty feet or so to the top of the tower. See, there are two or three steps remaining. The outside wall was a complete circular stone blank, there was no way for an enemy to obtain entrance. Of course the enemy's arrows and axes and fires would have been of no avail. There was just one low narrow door at the base, and it could have been easily locked from the inside, with thick stone bars.

People used to think the brochs were built by Picts, but the broch-builders were an earlier people than the Picts. And a very clever ingenious folk they must have been too . . .'

The school-children were bored stiff. For most of them, the broch was just a ruckle of stones . . . Bertie Williamson had slipped off and was down among the rockpools, half a mile along the shore, examining the life of tiny crabs and molluscs and delicate frail blossoms of seaweed. Two or three of the younger girls were filling their aprons with daisies, to be sweetly strung into neck-laces later . . . Jeremy Smith was watching his father's boat the *Willa May* coming in from the west on the first of the flood, followed by a flurry of gulls. His father must have had a good catch.

'Jeremy Smith,' said Mr Simon sharply, 'just refresh our minds. Tell us what this building was for, originally. Enlighten us, sir, from the depths of your archaeological wisdom.'

Jeremy Smith seemed to be having difficulty getting his thoughts into order. He had been dimly aware of Mr Simon's words through the images of the gull-flock, the baskets of sea-streaming mackerel in the *Willa May*, the surge and seethe of the Sound all about his father's boat, the two flashing knives wielded by Amos his father and Harry his older brother – indeed, once or twice the sun had caught the blade of the knife, though the *Willa May* was a mile off-shore, and made a little twinkle, a star, across the gray water.

'This ruin,' the boy managed to stammer at last, 'it was . . . I think . . . it must have been . . . let me see . . . a place where the Picts used to keep pigs . . .'

Mr Simon threw up his hands in despair . . . 'Pigs!' he

echoed. 'I have been casting my pearls before swine all morning. I almost despair. Are you not interested at all in your remote ancestors and the way they lived and the things they did? . . . Come, we'll go back to the school now and have one final geography lesson before the end of the summer term.'

Mr Simon noticed Bertie Williamson sitting on the rock-stack below, listening to the music of the incoming waters. 'You, sir,' yelled Mr Simon, 'how dare you! Come here at once. The tide's coming in. Do you want to be drowned, you dolt! Come up at once. We are returning to the school.'

Bertie Williamson let on not to hear Mr Simon's thin summons, for the crying of the gulls around the *Willa May*, and the rising sea-songs.

'That boy will feel the weight of my hand,' said Mr Simon. 'The longer he stays down there, the worse it'll be for him – summer holiday or no summer holiday . . .'

Mr Simon rounded up his flock and made a head-count. There was another boy missing, as well as Bertie Williamson.

It could only be Thorfinn Ragnarson, the dreamer.

There Thorfinn was, on the far outside wall of the broch, two thousand years lost in time.

*　　*　　*

The land seekers hauled up their ships. The islanders came down to meet them.

The bows of the sailors sang. A flock of arrows fell among the islanders.

The islanders snatched what they could from their huts and fled inland. Children danced, old men hobbled, women carried cheese presses and spinning whorls. They took to the hills. Most of their men lay dead or dying on the shore.

The men from the sea took possession of the village.

'Here is the place,' said the skipper. 'The land is fertile. A fish-fraught sea. Fowls on the cliff-ledges. Here we will settle.'

And they laid new stones of foundation.

And they broke up the ship that had carried them from the south, from Alba and Cornwall and Sicily, and made fishing boats.

And the dispossessed people living poorly among the hills: their shadows glimmered sometimes at dawn and sunset. And at night they came down stealthily and they killed a sheep or a sow or a calf.

So the migrant people, the strangers, established themselves on that shore.

But the ship that had taken them north to Orkney, 'the islands of the whale', was only one of a flock of ships.

Ship after ship anchored off this island and that, and the adventurers waded ashore and broke the native communities and took possession of the ploughlands and the sea banks.

To each island they gave a name.

They called one island Norday.

And the chief of each island said, 'Here is our land, after all the sea wanderings. Here we will live well, and our children's children after us.'

But it was not to be.

The sons and daughters of men do not live in peace for long.

The conqueror of the island of Selskay across the Sound from Norday was a formidable seaman and warrior. Selskay and all the new sea-lords of the Orkneys were known to each other; as wind-scattered seabirds know each others' ways; so these tribes had words and stories in common. The lord of Selskay sent men to the islands round about, with this message: 'You know how we are but branches from one great people, the first out-scatterings of a mighty northward-seeking wave, or little bee-swarms that have hived off here and there from the tumultuous golden mother-throng of bees. Other ships and other settlers will come, out of Donegal and Kintyre and Penzance, distant cousins, and seeing the green islands of Orc they will seek to possess them and drive us out, as we drove the dark people into the barren interior hills. So we must defend ourselves against the stronger children of the Sea King, when they come. But it will be no easy thing.'

And the chief of Norday, and all the other chiefs in the islands round about, agreed that they had no sure tenure of the lands and lochs and fishing-grounds they had taken.

And the Orkneymen agreed that it might go ill with them when the children of the Sea King – those more immediate to him than themselves (the first-comers, the mere spindrift of the mighty wave of migration) – came among them with their swifter ships and weapons of dark ringing iron.

'Yet,' said the unquiet lord of Selskay – a strong and subtle man in the assembly of the islands – 'it often hap-pens that a great common danger dredges out of a people an ingenuity they did not know they had.'

So those new Orkneymen ploughed their fields and fished and hunted, three generations and more, and they were not troubled, except that the moor-dwellers, the original dark people, came down in winter and took a sheep or a pig or a calf . . . If ever a sickness went like fire among the people, or a fishing boat was upset in a calm sea, or the barley-harvest was poor, then they said that of course the people of the moors and hills had put a dark enchantment on them.

Vagrants brought news from Ulster and Cumbria and Bute. The people in those places had been lately dispossessed by kindred tribes from further south; they had come suddenly in bigger ships and their axes had rung in the night, against the rocks and walls, like great black bells, and those stronger children of the Sea King had had little mercy on their cousins, the first invaders of a century earlier. They had had to seek refuge in the places of the whale and the eagle.

Once a Norday fisherman, casting lines far out in the west, saw one of those great ships sailing north along the horizon. That ship was on the very ocean rim, and could not have been seen from Norday or Selskay or Hrossey or any other of the Orkneys, being under the horizon. This solitary fisherman saw the ship, and how it seemed to hesitate, and its fine-woven sail fluttered, as though it smelt the sweet grasses and the peat-fires, and might decide to make landfall there. But then the skipper of this ship must have changed his mind, for the sail was set to catch the following wind, the ship held on northwards, towards Shetland or Iceland, and a silver wave spurted from her bow . . .

When news of this powerful questing ship was brought to Orkney, it seemed to the island chiefs that the shadow of death was upon them – their little communities were about to be broken and scattered as, five generations earlier, they had uprooted the original islanders, the dark people – the winter thieves and the sorcerers.

There was nothing they could do about it. The great

ship would come, this summer or that, the iron birds would fall among them, their bones would be broken, their fields and boats would be possessed by the distant southern cousins, the stronger children of the mighty Sea King.

Then the new ships would flock in upon the islands. They themselves would be only a memory. The dark people of the moors and the hills would be glad of it, in their underground chambers.

It was then that the magician of the stones and the circles rose in Orkney.

This builder wove together in one stone web, images – the upward spiral of the golden eagle, and the wheel of the sun, and the circle of a man's life, and the horizon rim, and the circuits of the fish shoals in the west, and the delicate house of the spider and the raven's rough nest in a crag ledge, and how the thistle-root surges slowly into the thistle-flower and delivers its airy thistledown again to the fruitful earth, in one pure wavering summerlong circle.

After the opening of quarries, the chiefs began to build their castles, towers, brochs, along the island shores.

The chief of Norday island said to the boy Thorfinn Ragnarson (you must understand, this was long before the time of the Vikings and the Norse settlers, and Thorfinn would have had a different name then, an early Celtic name long forgotten, but it was the same boy – that much is certain) 'Poet, this fort that our architect and masons are building so strong and true, it must be celebrated in a poem, or a dance of words, otherwise (though seemingly so solid) our tower can hardly be said to exist at all, all is but a shadow and a breath until the word invests it with strength and beauty. So, boy with the gift of language,

you are to make the Song of the Broch. Only, you understand, boy, you must order the poem as if it issued from
my mouth. I have no gift for language myself, but it carries
more authority if the poem seems to come from the lord
of the island. Make the poem soon, before the great ships
overshadow us. Do it well, boy, and you will not be the
poorer on account of it.'

So Thorfinn Ragnarson – under his early Celtic name
of course – made, that same day, the Song of the Broch.

THE SONG OF THE BROCH

Stone mother of this island, keep us well.
Mother, cast stone arms about us in a time of trouble.
Who will chide the axemen on the shore?
Who will drive those strangers, ashamed, off under
   the horizon?
The young lissom island mothers,
See, they wither at last, after many a good harvest
They are glad to be mingled with dust and rain,
And children weep for a day in the doorways.
You, stone mother, broch
You will see the withering of generations.
If a stone tear falls from you
At the passing of a hunter or a ploughman
It is not grief that the oldest and wisest can understand.
Great stone mother on the headland,
Let the enemy ships
Shrivel like moths in the fire of your mockery and
   rage.
You are stored with fish and cheeses for your children.
Sweet and pure your well water,
Beautiful your winding stair

Going up and round like the eagle, lost among clouds.
Stone mother, guardian
We will keep your stone coat always in good repair,
Replacing a worn stone with a quarried well-dressed
    stone.

Now we lay this honeycomb at your feet.
We make your feet shine
With water from a new rock-spring.

A boy has made a lustral song for you.
Do you dance? He who lies wakeful at midnight
Has known the beat and tremor of your strong
    powerful earth-fast feet.

Next summer, a ship of the Sea King came. The watchman
on the summit of the broch had seen the ship in the distance – at once he blew on his horn. It was anchored off
the island. The sailors, with their iron axes and iron-tipped
spears, began to wade ashore. The sea brimmed at their
throats, then at their shoulders, then at their waists and
ankles as they waded ashore, shaking bright drops from
them.

As soon as the ship had been sighted, the cowherd and
the shepherd had driven the flocks inland. The fishermen
had hidden the coracles and the creels in the caves at the
far end of the island.

Then the old chief herded the people in at the low
door of the broch, men and women and children, and they
brought with them into the broch as much smoked and
salted meat and fish as they could carry.

The broch had been so constructed that at the centre
of the floor a well had been sunk. At night a star shone

out of it. There seemed to be a perpetual song in the deep throat of the well.

The water, drawn up, was sweet and cold.

The invaders seemed puzzled that there was no sign of life in the village – no defiant voices or fists or spear-shakings down at the shore, no wailing flight of women and old folk and children inland; only this strange silent stone tower on the shallow cliff above the sea.

They walked up the sand, cautiously to begin with, fearing a trap. But there was no opposition at all. The village doors stood open, but the houses were empty of furnishings and food, nor were there boats on the beaches or beasts in the fields around.

It seemed that the island had been yielded without a blow. Their skipper said, 'We will live well in this fertile place.'

'Yes,' said a big black-bearded man who carried an axe with a curving blade, 'and we can store our sails and oars and sea-tackle in this tower above the Sound.'

'A pity, though,' said another sailor, 'that the cowards have left us no ale and cheese. We'll have to eat hard ships' biscuits till we get to know the fishing grounds.'

'No need to sail on any further,' said the skipper. 'Here is our place. We will build decent houses in place of the pigstyes where these islanders lived. It seems to me we could farm the place much better than them. Our people will live here many generations.'

'A spineless gutless folk,' said the black-bearded man. 'What cowards, to abandon their houses and fields without a fight!'

Then they heard a whirring like a great bird above their heads, and a stone came down suddenly and broke the shoulder of a young oarsman. There was such force in the flung stone that it bounced thrice on the ground under the tower.

The oarsman yelled and staggered and clutched at his shoulder.

The shipmen looked up. A dozen faces were looking down at them. 'Welcome, cousins from the sea,' said the watchman. 'Here are some more stones for you to build your own houses and barns . . .'

Then stones fell in a thunderous shower about the shipmen. The skull of one grizzled sailor was cracked like a nut. The others retreated out of range of the heavy stones.

'What cunning!' said the skipper. 'What treachery! This isn't fair fighting. They will pay dearly for this.'

The shipmen consulted down at the shore. How could they storm the tower? A round blank forty-foot-high wall stood there, with one low narrow door at the base.

'There's a storm cloud in the west,' said a voice from the tower. 'Why don't you come in, sea cousins, and shelter from the wind and the rain?'

There was laughter from inside the broch.

'You, Fergus,' said the skipper. 'I'm about to do you a great honour. You will go and kick open that door in the tower and we will come behind and so we'll get into the tower and deal with those ruffians.'

The man Fergus approached the tower holding his axe with the blunt hammer-head in front and he had to stoop at the low door in order to shatter the door with a blow. The axe was poised to strike when another bird whirred down – this time an arrow – and it went through the man's neck, and it quivered there for a while even after Fergus was lying dead.

The broch rang like a big stone bell with laughter and cheering.

'Laugh well,' shouted the skipper. 'I hear the high laughter of women. Laugh well, you hags. It will come soon to lamentation with you.'

Meantime the storm clouds had blown up in the west and the sun was hidden and the rain fell in sheets.

The shipmen had to take shelter under the cliffs. Even so, the cold rain was dripping from their beards.

'It's dry and warm in here,' said the voice from the tower. 'We are very comfortable. If you stretch your nostrils, you will soon get a fine smell of beef broth and broiled halibut. They are very good to eat with barley bread, especially washed down with ale from last winter.'

The shipmen's mouths shivered. They stilled the chattering of their teeth on dry sea biscuits.

Meantime very enchanting smells of cooking drifted down from the tower.

'I think,' said the black-bearded ruffian, 'we should go back to the ship and consider what we will do now. At least the sail will be an awning there against this thunder-burst.'

The skipper was looking across the Sound at the other islands within sight. Each one was guarded by a tall stone tower.

'They have sprung up everywhere in the north like mushrooms,' said the skipper. 'It may be difficult for us to get a foothold anywhere. We must hope that the knowledge of brochs hasn't reached Shetland or Faroe. Otherwise we might be condemned to be sea wanderers for the rest of time.'

The wind freshened. An edge of ice entered into the rain. A heavy hail shower rattled among the shore stones.

From inside the broch came the sound of a harp and a voice singing. It was the boy poet.

No more will the sea wolves trouble us.
Let the children of the Sea King
Find pasture in Lewis and Yell.
They should dig and drain like honest men
Till wilderness is cornland,
Not wander like thieves and murderers from coast to
    coast.
Then, in the age of peace,
We will exchange cargoes with them.
Then islanders and sailors
Will break bread, and laugh together at the tables.

Now the sky was covered all over with blue-black clouds. It looked as if the bad weather would go on for days.

The shipmen came out from under the inadequate shelter of the crags and walked down, splurging water, to the sea verge.

'A pity,' cried the old chief from the summit of the tower, 'that you couldn't stay a while longer, cousins of the Sea King.'

The skipper, seawater up to his knees, turned his face to the tower. 'Never fear,' he shouted. 'What cowards, hiding away in a stone beehive! We'll be back, tomorrow or next week or just when you're going to cut your barley. We'll come out of the blackness of night, you old gray coward, and that fortress of yours will be a strewment of stones along the links. Depend on it. This island and all the Orkneys will be ours!'

A great cheer went up from the broch when they saw

the last of the shipmen, oozing mingled sleet and sea-water, being hauled into the ship.

The archers in the tower sent a shower of valedictory arrows against the ship. Most of the arrows fell into the sea, but one struck the mast of the ship and clung there, thrumming.

After that Norday was troubled no more by seafarers.

They saw big ships on the horizon, from time to time, but those ships always sailed on north.

The boy made many poems next winter about the defeat of the sea-wolves, and those poems and songs were remembered in Orkney for generations.

Once the boy, gathering mussels from the ebb for the fishermen, saw a ship in the Sound, with a tattered sail and a few gaunt seamen.

The villagers gathered along the sea banks.

The six sailors came ashore. It turned out that they came from Norway in the east. It turned out that they too were of the same stock as the Orkneymen – only more distant children of the Sea King. They had certain words in common, still.

Bad harvests, oppression by the tribe in a neighbouring fjord, had driven these off-shore Norwegians westward. They had heard, they said, of rich arable lands in the west, where they and their children after them could live in peace. Alas! They were simple fisherfolk, unacquainted with the deeper waters, and so they had had a wretched voyage on the great ocean. And now, at the end of it all, there was no place for them. Every fertile patch on every island was occupied. There was no place for them to settle.

Those easterners had blue eyes and hair bright as the sun.

The lord of Norday gave them hospitality for one night, and a small store of dried fish and oatmeal. Also he saw to it that their water barrel was replenished.

'Sail on west still,' he told the Norwegians. 'We have heard stories of the islands of the west, where there are no such things as hunger, age, or death. It may be you will stumble on that beautiful shore.'

Next day the Norwegians rowed west, and now there seemed to be energy and urgency in their oar-strokes.

'We have nothing to fear from Norway,' said the islanders.

Some of the women of Norday said they had never seen more handsome men than those easterners.

'It seems to me,' said the old lord, 'that once those men of Norway learn sea-skills, they will become formidable sailors. We must hope, for the sake of our children, that they will be content among their own mountains and fjords.'

The boy poet made a song about the islands in the Western Ocean.

After a few peaceful years, the tower began to be neglected somewhat.

A winter tempest dislodged one of the high stones. It lay where it had fallen, on the shore, until at last the waves ground it to sand.

*　　*　　*

A stone had fallen from the truncated broch. It trundled on to the rocks below.

Was it that stone that woke Thorfinn, or Mr Simon's voice? 'So there you are, you miserable wretch, playing

89

truant again, two days before the summer holiday. I wonder what I should do – give you four of the strap . . . No, you will write out a hundred times, *I will not dream during lessons again* . . .'

The Muse

THERE WERE ONLY two big houses in the island – the
minister's Manse and the laird's Hall, the latter built in
the eighteenth century, much added to in the nineteenth
century with Gothic tower and battlements, and a little
chapel with stained glass windows. (The lairds had always
been Episcopalians.)

The original Hall had been burned down in 1746 by
sailors from one of King George II's ships, because the
then laird had sympathized openly with the Jacobite
Rebellion, and the poor man, along with several other
supporters of Bonnie Prince Charlie, had had to winter
in a cave in the island of Westray ('the gentlemen's ha'')
and had come home to a burnt-out shell. He had died a
year later of acute bronchial trouble, got from that dread-
ful winter in the cave, with no port wine or sea-coal fires
or roast beef to keep the bleak airs and sea spray out of
his system.

How Thorfinn Ragnarson, hearing this story, had
wished to be in that rebellion, following the handsome

young prince from the West Highlands (his landfall from
France) to his victory over Sir John Cope's Hanoverian
army at Prestonpans, the occupation of Edinburgh and
the balls and levees at Holyrood, then the surge across
the Borders and into England; so that King George the
German upstart trembled on his throne and the London
grandees and wealthy merchants began to cram their
trunks with silver and precious deeds and documents, and
chartered ships to take them to the Low Countries . . .
Alas, the story turned out badly, because at Derby, almost
within sight of triumph for the true and ancient house of
Stuart, Prince Charles Edward was advised to turn back
– the odds against him were too strong – a huge army
was being mustered to stand between his brave Highland
soldiers and London. At the end of the long retreat back
to Scotland, the prince's army had been blown to pieces
by the cannon and savagely massacred by the bayonets of
the Duke of Cumberland, 'the butcher' as he was known
ever afterwards . . . The boy of Ingle croft dreamed often
of accompanying the prince on his perilous flight among
the mountains, lochs, and islands, pursued by the English
redcoats, with a massive ransom on his head . . . Never
had the courtesy and loyalty of the Highlanders shone so
bright as in that dark time – never had the prince and his
band of followers been happier, there among the mists
and snows and stormy firths of the west . . . Eventually
the prince got away in a French ship, to a long life of exile,
disappointment, dependency on French kings, alcoholism
and death. (True, he was called King Charles III by his
dwindling band of Stuart adherents, but what an empty
title as he received his few 'courtiers' in Rome in a coat
with frayed silk sleeves, and features coarsened by late-
night drinking and card playing!) The idle useless boy of

Norday, Thorfinn Ragnarson, refused to follow the idle useless Bonnie Prince Charlie, in imagination, to his final seedy bourne . . . Better by far, in hindsight, if the prince had fallen among his brave clans on the moor at Culloden, that bitterly cold April morning in 1746, with rain clouds blowing across the battlefield . . . Thorfinn went so far as to imagine a glorious death for himself near the red thunderous throat of a Hanoverian cannon . . . But then, a lark singing above the laird's Hall, he was very glad to be alive. Oh very glad indeed! – a curlew was calling across the fields, the heads of seven seals were bobbing beside the reef, a new calf was 'gazing out of silly eyes at a hundred mysteries', across the ditch there . . . Faint it trembled on the wind, the school bell. The idle useless pupil was late again . . . Thorfinn slung his school bag over his shoulder and got to his feet.

There, against the surging blue and white of the sky (for it was a windy morning) the girl who was staying at the minister's (whoever she was) rode the laird's chestnut, her yellow hair streaming out behind her. The girl and the horse climbed the peat track to the summit of the hill Fea.

The girl must have caught sight of the schoolboy, for she reined in the young horse, and waved to him from a dozen fields away. As she called to him – her voice came thin and sweet on the wind.

Thorfinn ran on towards the village school, and to Mr Simon's ridicule and Mr Simon's contemptuous punch on the shoulder as he sent him to his desk, yet once more.

But even as he ran, Thorfinn wondered about the girl on horseback – it was well known that nobody rode that horse but the laird's granddaughters when they came from their English public schools to spend the summer in Norday.

Mr Simon was devoting a period to Greek and Roman myth that day. Pegasus the winged horse of poetry came into it, along with Zeus and Aphrodite and the Minotaur . . . The image of the girl on the horse glowed and faded in his mind all morning . . . A rough and tumble of football in the playground broke the image at last. He thought no more about it – he was glad – he decided he did not like girls; not even his sisters Inga, Sigrid, and Ragna . . .

Who wants to hear about a lazy idle boy? We are talking about important people in the island, Mr Harcourt-Smithers the laird and Revd Hector Drummond and their two big houses, the Hall and the Manse, that dominated the island of long low crofts and modest farm steadings.

The laird was an elderly widower, a pleasant inarticulate old man in a rough tweed suit and a deerstalker who lived most of the year in London and only came to Norday in summer for the trout fishing and the grouse shooting. The huge house of his ancestors, with twenty rooms and stable and summer house and chapel, was slowly rotting on its foundations, for lack of firing and airing. In Victorian times, when it was in its heyday, a troop of girl servants would have seen to the fires, the scouring of the plenteous silverware, the dusting of Queen Anne chairs and Morris hangings . . . Those days were long past; the laird's rent-roll was much truncated; to pay death duties his grandfather (who had owned the whole of Norday from the lowest stone in the ebb to the topmost cairn-stone on the summit of Fea) had had to sell nearly every farm and croft in the island, and then cheaply enough, for none of the islanders was well off.

Nowadays Thomas Vass his factor – who also was coal-merchant and seed-merchant and a shareholder in the inter-island steamer *Raven* – and county councillor also – called at the Hall once a week or so in winter to see if the roof, or any windows and doors, needed urgent repairs, and to lay down rat poison for the rodents that kept finding their way in through fissures in the cellar and the stable wall.

The garden – once tended by two faithful gardeners – was a jungle of weeds. Thomas Vass refused point blank to have anything to do with the high-walled garden except to take a scythe to the long grass when the laird and his two granddaughters were expected in late June.

The two-year-old chestnut colt, called Selkie, Mr Vass kept in his own yard all the rest of the year.

One summer day the factor-merchant would receive a telegram – 'Arriving off steamer tomorrow, Harcourt-Smithers'. Isa Estquoy wrote out the telegram, and put it in its buff envelope and the whole island knew before Thomas Vass that the laird and his granddaughters were on their way – were, even then, steaming on the train across the desolate moor of Sutherland between the lonesome stations of Forsinard and Altnabreac, and would soon be on the stormy Pentland Firth, with the great purple island of Hoy on one side and the low green Scapa Flow islands on the other. Then, by taxi and another steamer, the *Raven*, to the island where their remote ancestors, the Viking settlers from Norway, had first drawn up their longships. (Or so they claimed; in fact the family had only been in Orkney for three centuries, and the original – a retainer of Earl Patrick Stewart – a ruffian and a lickspittle from Fife in Scotland – had gotten the rents and revenues of Norday for his faithful service to

Earl Patrick . . . There was more original Norse blood in Jimmo Greenay the beachcomber and Howie Ayre the quarryman than ever flowed in the veins of Mr Harcourt-Smithers the laird.)

But let that be. The present Mr Harcourt-Smithers was a stout red-faced kindly humorous inarticulate man, liked by nearly all the islanders except for such levellers as Ben Hoy and Simon the schoolmaster and MacTavish the innkeeper. Whenever Mr Harcourt-Smithers spoke, the phrases came in short bursts, with long struggling silences in between, during which he tried to indicate his meaning with strenuous gestures and jerkings of the head – and that mime language was generally more understood than the brief word spasms (the vocables of Eton and Oxford have always been a strange music to the islanders, especially when delivered in the eccentric style of the laird).

Anyway, the harmless old gentleman was expected, himself and his two young granddaughters. Thomas Vass would read the telegram, then drive his old Ford – the only car in the island at that time – to the Hall, throw open all the windows, and light fires in the dining-room, the sitting-room, and two bedrooms. Then he would take his scythe to the long grass, and open the stable door to receive the chestnut colt, Selkie.

But, this particular summer, the old laird came alone on the *Raven*'s small boat to the slipway of the island.

Thomas Vass gave him a civil greeting and carried his cases up the pier and stowed them in the boot of his car.

'No girls this year,' said Mr Harcourt-Smithers. 'No Debbie. No Penny. School now . . . No time for their old grandfather . . . Gone to some place in Ireland with school friends . . . Can't be helped . . . Changes every-

where . . . Manage somehow . . . Thanks, Vass, very
good of you . . . Dunno what to do with that young horse
. . . We'll see, we'll see . . . Some brandy and port wine
in the cupboard, is there . . . ? Might as well have a bite
of lunch in the inn later . . . A scoundrel, that chap
MacTavish . . . Outrageous what he charges for his
whisky . . . No war, there won't be any war, something'll
be sorted out with the Germans . . . Russians and Yanks,
they're the ones to look out for . . . Old country's got
some life in it yet, the lion can lash its tail, they'll see . . .
Car must be pretty old now, Vass, eh? . . . There's the
Manse, is that weird minister fellow still there, what's-his-
name, Drummond? Strange fellow altogether. Hold on –
is that a young woman there, in his garden, weeding? . . .
Maybe not, thought I saw someone, strange . . . You look
older this year, Vass, you worry too much, too much
getting and spending, want to take it easy . . . Don't know
what to do about that horse, now Debbie and Penny won't
be coming any more. A worry . . . Oh yes, Vass, you can
show me the rent ledger sometime, no hurry . . . I expect
you all swindle a poor old man like me right and left. You
too, Vass. But I don't worry . . . Dear me, haven't spoken
so much for a long time, it's the air, Vass, the sea air and
the wind in the oatfields . . . Plenty of fine sheep this
year. Coats like silk on them cows . . . This island makes
me poetical, damn foolish talk, but I like being home. I
like it. Can't help it . . . Soon as we dump the luggage,
Vass, drive me down to the inn for a bite of lunch. You're
welcome to eat with me. No? Wife has stewpot on . . .
Oh, well, I had a wife once, a stickler for punctuality. I
miss her, Vass, miss her terribly . . . She used to like it
here, more than I did, even more than me . . . Kept the
old place in good heart, Lucy. Must visit Lucy's grave on

the hill before sunset. Always do that. Won't be long till
I'm lying there myself. Can't come too soon, I think to
myself some days. Ah well . . . The granddaughters, pale
shadows of Lucy, God rest her . . . Let me see, that croft
on the hillside, what do they call it, Smylder? . . . Amazed
that old man's still alive, what's-his-name, Olafson . . .
Did you see that, Vass, he shook his fist at the car as we
went by . . . Awkward old blighter . . . Is that socialist
fellow still the teacher? Filling children's heads with nonsense . . . Who could she have been, that beautiful young
person in the minister's garden? I expect I imagined her.
The loveliness everywhere today . . . Never saw Norday
in such good heart . . . Nearly didn't come, though, this
year. Debbie and Penny letting me down like that . . .
Well, here we are, Vass, thank you . . . Hasn't exactly
changed for the better, my noble pile, has it, Vass? . . .
Great chunk of plaster out of the south gable. Slates slip-
ping . . . Do my time, though, it'll do my time . . . could
almost hunt tigers in my garden now, eh? What to do
with this horse though – what's-his-name, Selkie – see, he
won't take a fistful of clover from me, Vass . . . They can
smell decay, death . . . Smarter than us, horses and dogs,
in many ways . . . Don't want to sell it. Can't shoot it. A
lovely creature, though . . . Thank you, Vass. Enjoyed
the ride . . . Look, Vass, something for your trouble, yes,
a sovereign. Don't see many of them gold coins nowadays.
Take it, man . . . A swig, Vass. Have a swig out of my
flask, celebrate the homecoming. Good stuff, Old
Orkney whisky . . . Had a few swigs on the boat –
what's-its-name, *Raven* – coming over. Maybe that's why
I'm speaking so much . . . That and the great joy I feel
– no other word for it, Vass, no other word – at being
home again . . . For an hour or two, coming back home,

I know what it feels like, being a poet . . . Just listen to that lark! . . . So that's that, Vass . . . If you'll be so good now as to drive me to the inn, see if I can get a bite of lunch from that scoundrel . . . Good malt, eh, Vass. Have another swig. Drive all the better for it . . . Better get some provisions, too . . . Still alive, is she, Isa what's-her-name? . . . There's that old beachcomber fellow coming up from the shore with a something in his sack. Stop the car a minute, would you, Vass . . . I'd like to give what's-his-name, the beachcomber, Jimmo Greenay, a taste of this good malt . . . Good old Greenay, good old Norday, I feel very happy today . . . Got gout, got angina, short in the puff, and happy to be home . . . What does the bard say? – "this precious stone set in a silver sea" . . . Hits it off exactly . . . Ho, Jimmo Greenay! Come here a minute, my friend. I want you to take a sup from my flask . . .'

So the old laird, Mr Harcourt-Smithers, came back alone to spend his two summer months in his island . . .

He spoke more that morning than he did for all the rest of his time in Norday.

*　　*　　*

To the only other big house in the island, the Manse, two winters before, had come the minister, Reverend Hector Drummond, from being an assistant at a big church in Glasgow.

The island had had eccentric pastors for generations, a few of them scholars and amateur scientists (botanists and archaeologists). One minister in the late eighteenth century read only the Latin poets – poets like Pope and Wordsworth he dismissed; even Shakespeare was a barbarian with flashes of talent, 'but no form, no purity of

shape to properly contain his undoubted inspirations . . .'
Another minister had written a voluminous history of the
islands, and he had discerned, first of all through the mists
of time, the forgotten earls and saints and heroes of medi-
eval Orkney. He guessed that the fishermen and farmers
with their blond beards and blue eyes were the descend-
ants of the Norwegian settlers, a thousand years back in
time . . . One minister in the Napoleonic era had bitterly
chided the young island men for not volunteering for His
Majesty's men-of-war. 'No,' he cried from the pulpit,
purple-faced, 'you desert your King and country in their
hour of need, you enrol for the Davis Straits whale-
fishing, or the Hudson's Bay fur-trade among the savage
Indians, you run to hide like cowards in caves and crannies
and cellars. Think shame of yourselves. A cowardly heart
in a young man makes pitiful and wretched his old age,
no matter what wealth he has stored for himself . . .' All
this at a time when the thugs of the press-gang were
dragging young men from the ploughs and fishing-boats,
into those hell-ships . . . A later minister still had wandered along the shore, year after year, with a hammer,
breaking pieces off a cliff-face here and a reef there, so
that most of the islanders thought he couldn't be quite
right in the head. But then this minister would travel to
Kirkwall, to meetings of the Antiquarian Society there,
and he would lay out his stone fragments before the other
members. And lo! each stone, like a leaf in the book of
Creation, showed a black fish, or a frond of seaweed, or
a scallop shell, preserved and petrified there from the
beginnings of time. How long? A Bishop Usher had put
the date of Creation at 4004 BC. The Society members
looked at each other with a wild surmise; surely those
fossils must be older, very much older! The mid-

nineteenth century minister of Norday would not commit himself. 'I have picked up a few curious things from the shore of the great ocean of time,' was all he would say. 'Depend upon it, there are other greater mysteries waiting to be found. God's creation is more wonderful than some of us have hitherto believed.'

Those ministers had all been married men, a few of them with large families. Their extra-clerical activities had by no means interfered with their ministries. Some of them had been strict and puritanical, and young men and women seeing them on the road would turn aside up a sheep-path or down a track to the shore, for some of the Old Kirk ministers did not confine their thunders to the pulpit on the Sabbath . . . Others were kindly indulgent men, well loved by most of the islanders; and if a nod and a wink might pass between a minister and the innkeeper, concerning the nocturnal delivery at the back door of the Manse of a case of brandy – possibly smuggled from a Dutch ship at moon-dark – nobody minded, except maybe the lady of the Manse (and she did not have a key to every cupboard in that large dwelling).

In general, the minister's wife was the ruler of the household and the family, and she regulated the comings and goings of those eccentric pastors. They saw to it that their husbands ate two substantial meals a day. If the archaeologist minister picked up his hammer and his magnifying glass and his little leather bag some fine afternoon, she would say quite firmly, 'It's Thursday, Charles, sermon-writing time . . .' He might brush past her to be down in the ebb before the tide turned, if the scientific frenzy was on him, but mostly he bowed to his good lady's strict regime. How else could a manse and a parish be well ordered?

101

So it went on, up to the nineteen-thirties, minister succeeding minister, till old Mr Aberneǐthy retired and went to live with his widowed daughter in Arbroath. There had been nothing remarkable about Mr Abernethy, except that he was passionate against 'strong drink', and so there came a kind of schism in the life of Norday – the inn versus the kirk – a situation that had not been known before. Mr Abernethy had even attempted to have the bar of the inn closed down, by invoking a Victorian act of parliament and campaigning to have the island voted 'dry'. And he had come within twenty-one votes of succeeding! The farmers and fishermen – most of them – blenched that evening when the result of the abolitionist poll was announced. What! – never to have a dram again on the day of the agricultural show, or on the New Year rounds of masquing and chanting. Never to wash the salt from their throats when they came back from the west in their yoles – never to wash down the golden dust of harvest! It had almost happened, and that old Abernethy up in the Manse had been to blame. From that day there began to be a decline in kirk attendance, mostly amongst the men-folk (though many continued faithful, in spite of all).

It had been the women of Norday who had rallied round the Revd Aeneas Abernethy's temperance banner, all through the campaign. The wives and mothers and sisters had got tired at last, after generations and centuries, of sitting at home on winter nights, wondering how the bairns and themselves were to be fed and clothed, while the men poured all the meagre profit of land and sea down their throats in that den of iniquity in the village – next-door to the kirk itself. (Not all, or even a majority, of the island breadwinners behaved in this disgraceful way

– they saw to it that nothing was lacking in cupboard or hearth, or in the way of protection against storm in tight-thatched roof and stout shutter; some of them even put by a penny a week to pay for a funeral, in case of any mortal mischance. But most saw in a dram or a mug of beer the just rewards of their toil by land and sea – and moreover it gave them the freedom of legend and song, loosed for an hour or two from the grinding cycle of labour. They drank moderately and they were religious men, a few of them elders: 'We observe temperance in the true sense of the word', said Willum Holm of the farm of Pools, and an elder, gravely. He had voted 'wet' on that momentous day; and though he did his kirk-elder's duties punctiliously afterwards, there was a lasting coldness between himself and Mr Abernethy.)

Of course there were a few young men who couldn't hold their drink. Folk going to kirk on the Sabbath would sometimes see one or other of those wasters lying dead drunk in the ditch. There was no doubt too, that a few families did suffer because the man of the house spent most of his earnings at the bar counter. And it was well known that in some crofts – one or two only, thank goodness – there would be occasional violence. Shouting and pleading and the crying of children would be heard on still summer nights – breaking of chairs and crockery – and some young wife not daring to show herself at kirk or grocery van till the blue-black swelling was fading from her eye, till there was only a faint scar at her bloodied mouth . . . And on one occasion at least a drunken oaf of a boy had upset the oil lamp on his parents' dresser, and but for the neighbour men with their sticks and chain of water buckets from the croft well, the dwellers in that house would have had to wander at the mercy

103

of the elements – probably seek refuge at last in the dreaded 'poor house' in Kirkwall . . . Of course the *Raven* came back every August from Lammas Market Day in Kirkwall with its freight of tipsy islanders, who would then make their various ways home staggering and singing and behaving like clowns or masquers out of some mad melodrama.

It was the aggregate of all those things that came within an ace of giving triumph to the temperance party in Norday.

The 'inn faction' had just managed to hold on by their fingernails. But there weren't quite such wild alcoholic incidents as formerly.

Even if the worst had come to the worst, anyone who wanted a bottle of 'Old Orkney' could have had it sent from the town on the *Raven*. And, pub or no pub, there were a good half-dozen crofts in Norday where excellent ale was brewed; 'better' the brewing women would say, 'than that chemical trash they serve along at the inn down there . . .'

So, for almost a generation, that was the serious social cleavage in the island, the inn-folk against the kirk-folk – but even there the dividing line was very much blurred. Some of the inn-frequenters went so far as to say that Revd Abernethy had cases of whisky delivered to him from Leith, under pretext that the cases contained hymn-books; and, said Andrew Rosey who delivered one consignment at the Manse, 'your hymn-books are leaking, sir, and they're smelling of Johnny Walker . . .' But Andrew Rosey the ferryman was well known as an inventor of episodes, and in general he was disbelieved, even by the men round the pub fire.

*　　*　　*

At last, in 1935, the Revd Aeneas Abernethy retired. After due process of interview by the kirk session, selection, call, induction, a young assistant minister from Glasgow came to live in the Manse and attend to the flock of Norday souls. Soon the islanders realized that they had another eccentric minister, but one who was not a burden to them: Revd Hector Drummond.

The islanders knew of course that he was a bachelor, but they expected, and rather hoped, that soon he would go away south briefly and bring back a wife, for there had never been a bachelor minister in Norday before. But he lived alone in the Manse two winters and a summer and there was never any word of a bride, a lady of the Manse to look after him and preside over the monthly meetings of the Women's Guild. Some of the kirk folk tried, by devious ways, to discover if the new minister was betrothed, or likely to be betrothed, in the not too distant future, but Revd Hector Drummond let on not to understand their drift, and answered with a grave look, or a smile, or an answer that had nothing to do with matrimony.

Yes, but surely he ought to have a housekeeper – there were plenty of able women who would cook for him and clean the Manse and do his laundry and weed the tattie patch and the flower borders. Nothing doing – the weeks and months passed and the new minister didn't even enquire about a housekeeper, or even some capable lass who might come once or twice a week to sweep the cobwebs and shine the tall windows.

After a year, the Manse began to look very grubby, from the outside at least. What confusion and filth must be indoors then? Nobody ever got to know, because the minister never entertained visitors in the Manse. Even if the session clerk called about some pressing church

business, Revd Hector Drummond discussed the letters or
the account book with him in the lobby, and with the front
door open, whatever the weather outside. If it was some
complicated business, the minister would say mildly, 'Why
don't we discuss it in the vestry after evening service on
Sunday, Mr Taing? It's a bit draughty here in the lobby.'

So off Simon Taing, farmer of the Bu and session clerk,
would have to go, off and out into the wind and rain, with
his urgent letters in his pocket, to cycle back home.

'A queer fellow,' said Simon Taing to the men in the
smithy, 'but you can't help liking him.'

Even the agnostics and the rationalists in the smithy,
and in the pub, had to agree that the minister was all
right, nothing wrong with him, as far as things went. 'But,'
said Ben Hoy with the froth of a new pint in his whiskers,
'it's all nonsense, of course, no need of kirks or ministers
at all, the time's not far off when the human race'll rid
itself of superstition once and for all, and that time can't
come soon enough. Don't forget, it isn't that long ago
since they tried to shut the pubs here and everywhere else
in Scotland . . . This one, Drummond, he's tarred with
the same brush, make no mistake, though I suppose he's
all right to pass the time of day with . . .'

More seriously, from the women's point of view, Revd
Hector didn't seem to be eating at all. He visited Isa
Estquoy's shop only once a week, and that was to buy a
loaf of bread and a half-pound of Stork margarine and
(occasionally) a tin of Tate & Lyle's Golden Syrup; and
he always bought two three-ha'penny stamps on a Saturday to stick on the two letters he posted every Monday
morning, one (Isa Estquoy presumed) to his mother in
Kelso, one, a postcard, to a Miss Sophia Lauderdale in
Edinburgh (but there was nothing romantic whatever on

106

the postcard, it was a farrago of childish jokes and word-play that Isa Estquoy could make nothing of at all . . . silly nonsense).

The minister visited the farms and crofts regularly, and he seemed to enjoy very much the cakes, shortbread and scones that were set before him.

'The poor man, I wonder he doesn't burst, eating buns and drinking tea six times in an afternoon,' said Isa Estquoy. Bella Simpson thought this was his main nourishment, what he ate on his pastoral rounds; only those tidbits and tea out of the best china plates and cups brought out only for superior visitors.

Certainly Mr Drummond looked thin and pale and unkempt, in winter especially when his hollow cheeks seemed to hold the gray January shadows.

His boots had only a half-hearted gleam on them, and the sleeves of his dark ecclesiastical jacket were frayed.

Some of the ladies of the Women's Guild, six months or so after he came among them, offered to clean the Manse for him occasionally, and wash his sheets. In the gentlest way possible, Mr Drummond declined their kind offers. He was managing quite well, he said.

The shirt and underwear he hung out to dry in his weed-flourishing garden had had small soap and less kneading worked into them. Gray shapes, they flapped in the wind and rain.

'I tell you what it is,' said Tina Lyde, 'He's a miser. He hoards every ha'penny of his three hundred pounds a year.'

It seemed to be so, indeed. Thomas Vass the merchant and factor complained that no coal was ever delivered to the Manse from his store. The peat-cuttings that went with the Manse were uncut in May, both years. But after a westerly gale Mr Drummond might be seen coming up from the beach, in the early morning, laden with drift-wood. 'He'll never comb white hairs, that minister,' said Bella Simpson in the village shop. 'He'll be found some morning lying stiff in that cold cavern of a manse.'

The farm wives and the fish wives would present themselves from time to time at the Manse door with cheese, eggs, bannocks, butter, fish. He accepted the gifts courteously. An hour or so later he would be seen down at Jimmo Greenay's hut at the shore, giving the food to that lazy good-for-nothing.

After once or twice of that, the good women of Norday came no more to the Manse with gifts.

'He spends more time with little-use folk than he does with respectable folk like us,' said Isa Estquoy in the shop, quite indignantly. (Isa Estquoy played the organ on Sundays.)

It was quite true. He would linger talking a strucken hour with the tinkers at the roadside, even though the tinkers were Catholics who had come originally from Ireland at the time of the great potato famine.

The ladies of the Women's Guild tut-tutted, many of them. It wasn't good enough. Things were going a bit too far.

Mr Drummond tried to heal the rift between the kirk-folk and the inn-folk, that had lasted a quarter of a century. One night in winter he appeared in the pub, a thing never known before. The drinkers froze. 'Good evening, MacTavish,' said the minister. 'Be so good as to fill the men's glasses, whisky or beer, whatever they want. Then tell me what it comes to. And I'll have a glass of ginger ale myself . . .'

The men raised brimming mugs and glasses to the

minister, and drank rather more strenuously than they would have done if this particular visitant hadn't been there. But where there had been, ten minutes before, a tumultuous babble of voices, now there was an uneasy silence, only a throat being cleared here and there. A few men – Jock Seatter the blacksmith and Ben Hoy the sailor – approached the minister and exchanged a few stumbling words, but soon went back to the bar. And Mr Drummond stood there alone by the door at last.

'A few of you don't come to the kirk,' said the minister, 'so I thought I'd visit you instead. I would be glad to know you better.'

Then he threw back his glass of ginger ale, raised his hand to them all, and went out into the wind and rain.

When they heard that news the next morning, in Isa Estquoy's shop, the island women were outraged. 'A *minister*, in a *pub*! . . .' 'I sometimes wonder about him – you know – if he's all right in the top storey . . .' 'He only drank ginger beer though, I heard . . .' 'Yes, but a *minister*, in a *pub* . . .'

There was no getting past it, Revd Hector Drummond was eccentric. After two winters and a summer of his incumbency, most of the islanders were reconciled to it.

Even the sternest women, in time, were pleased when he came on his quarterly visitation round, and so obviously enjoyed their rhubarb-jam scones and fruit cake. He seemed always like a messenger who had come to visit the crofts from a far country, bringing pleasant tidings (though his boots were caked in month-old mud and salt, and once more he had made a botch of shaving: a scatter of tiny cuts all over his ascetic face).

Most of the kirk-going men declared that his sermons were good, neither too long nor too short, and sound doctrine. 'A good man, a very fine man,' said Simon Taing the session clerk, 'and we're none of us perfect.'

Mr Drummond came into his own at christenings and funerals.

At the font, his face shone with joy as he let fall the water-drops on the head of the new little islander. Even though the bairn yelled lustily, there was a solemn happiness among the congregation that a healthy full-lunged future ploughman or fisherman had been given to them.

And at all island funerals there was no lugubriousness, no masks of woe. But it was as if their minister was sending the dead person out on the last voyage, into timelessness, with a blessing on him or her, after the brief vain hucksterings of time. In the kirkyard, at a funeral, even the coarsest islander was touched with a certain awe and wonderment.

*   *   *

There was, that second spring of Mr Drummond's incumbency, the episode of the strange young woman. She arrived off the *Raven*, the steamer that served the islands, carrying a heavy suitcase. The *Raven* anchored off-shore – passengers and beasts and freight were rowed ashore on the ship's boat.

No one was there, on the slipway of Norday, to greet her.

She was a beautiful girl, with a great mass of golden hair and smart city clothes. She greeted the loafers on the pier cheerfully. They gaped at her, as at some rare exotic bird. She turned and waved goodbye to the crew of the *Raven*, and those dour men smiled, and the engineer went so far as to blow her a kiss, and Simpson the skipper took his pipe out of his mouth and spat into the sea (that was

Simpson's way of showing his appreciation of someone or something).

Tina Lyde and a few other women lingered at the top of the pier, speculating about the stranger. They always gathered there, when the *Raven* called. Who was she? What business had she on the island? Ah, she must be some descendant of the old laird – but in that case why hadn't Mr Harcourt-Smithers sent down Thomas Vass in his stuttering stinking old Ford to greet her?

The women of Norday whispered, nodded, gave askance looks.

'A beautiful morning,' cried the girl, and Tina Lyde at least recognized the accent of Edinburgh – one of the better-class districts, Morningside maybe. (Tina Lyde had been a servant to an Orkney-born skipper in Leith for a time, ten years before.)

She could only be staying at the inn, then; and she would be poorly housed there, because MacTavish didn't really want guests and all the work of cooking for them, and cleaning their rooms. (MacTavish was too mean to employ a well-handed local girl, and if he had had a good menu and bright swept airy bedrooms, the few tourists who did come to Norday might have stayed longer than a night or two. MacTavish was only interested in serving spirits and ales to the locals, and Mabel the occasional barmaid was miserably paid. But if the stranger was going to be a guest at the inn, MacTavish or Billy Holm his odd-job man would surely have been at the slipway, to help her off the *Raven*'s boat with her luggage.)

'Heave-ho!' cried the girl, and went lurching up the pier, all weighted down on one side with her heavy case. She walked through the village, sometimes setting her case down to take a breather . . . Then she climbed the

111

brae to the Manse. She set down the case at the doorstep and opened the heavy door and called, 'Hector, you brute, why weren't you meeting me!'

And there was Revd Hector Drummond, a shaving brush in his hand and his face half coated in lather. 'I forgot you were coming today, I clean forgot.' Then he kissed his visitor, and her face took a blotch of shaving-soap.

The girl laughed and gave him a kiss on his unlathered cheek, and they went inside and closed the door . . .

There was something passing strange about it, the chorus of island women considered. Who could this woman be? Had the minister decided at last to get a housekeeper? But you don't daub a newly-employed housekeeper's face with shaving soap, far less kiss her.

Ah, she must be some niece or other, come to visit her uncle in his Manse. ('Poor lass, she'll have a miserable holiday in that gloomy place . . .')

The women of Norday tried, in the course of the next week or two, by devious ways, to find out more about this young woman, but they got no satisfaction, however delicately they tried.

At last, after three days of mystery, Millie Smith chanced to see out of her gable window the minister walking down to the village. She was there, at her garden gate, as he passed.

'Isn't it good weather we're having?' she said. 'I'm glad for your niece's sake. All this sun and fresh air will set her up for the winter.'

The minister touched the brim of his hat. 'It is a fine morning,' he said, 'and I don't have a niece.'

And on he went.

If she wasn't a niece, who could she be? She was too young to be his sister, surely. A shiver of excitement went through the island women. There was only one explanation – Mr Drummond's fiancée! They were engaged to be married. Soon there would be a lady at the Manse. 'And not before time. He'll be decently turned out. He'll get a bit of solid flesh on his bones. The dirty Manse windows'll be shining soon. The roses and lupins in the garden will bloom like they used to do in Mrs Abernethy's time . . .'

But a few of the younger women weren't all that pleased. Maybe one or two of them had had hopes of being the lady of the Manse.

But if she wasn't a niece, what was she doing staying unchaperoned up there with a bachelor minister? It wasn't right, surely. What was all the secrecy for? They didn't even know her name.

The nameless girl sometimes came to the village with a basket for messages: and now the Manse basket was laden, when she left, with eggs, butter, cheese, honey, and oatmeal . . . 'It must be breaking his heart to part with all that money,' said Isa Estquoy later to the village women in the shop.

If only they knew her name!

'I hope you're enjoying your holiday, Miss – oh, I didn't catch your name . . .'

'I am not here on holiday,' said the stranger. 'I'll be going up the hill and along the cliffs this afternoon, as soon as Hector's had his dinner. He eats no more than a bird.'

A few women were in the shop now, like bees hovering about a blossom. Not on holiday? Going up the hill? Along the cliffs . . .

There was something a little unsettling, even sinister, about it.

The anonymous guest at the Manse bade the women a 'good morning', very pleasantly, and left the post office.

Tina Lyde wondered whether somebody oughtn't to write to the General Assembly about it – or at least to the Presbytery in Kirkwall.

It was the very end of winter when the girl had arrived. The last of the snow was melting from the sides of the hill dykes, and the first snowdrops had come and gone in the little gardens of Norday, and the crocuses lay here and there in the grass like small pieces of stained glass. But the bitter wind blew through winter's end, and the old folk said in the doorways, 'As the day lengthens, the cold strengthens.'

Then suddenly, almost overnight, the daffodils arrived, at first singly or in little groups, and then the whole island was thronged with the yellow flames on the long green tapers. Winter hurled at the daffodils last showers of hail – they danced in the gray wind, as if equally blessed by snow and sun.

Most of the girl's days seemed to be spent along the shore or the crag-tops. She carried binoculars. Sometimes she made a note in a little book she kept in her pocket.

One morning she had a mug of tea from Jimmo the beachcomber in his hut – a risky thing to do, for Jimmo never washed his mugs . . . Her laughter rang along the shore. Jimmo, when he came to the inn an hour later for his half pint, looked as happy as a school boy, through the ingrained salt and grime on his face.

And once, going up the hill, she stood at the door of Smylder and spoke for a while to old Jacob Olafson – a thing hardly known before, for Jacob usually growled low

114

in his throat if it seemed that anyone at all wanted to linger. They spent a full half-hour together, very agreeably, it seemed to those observing from the dozen croft windows around. Jacob even passed his box of snuff to the girl, and she actually snuffed and vented three shattering sneezes. 'That's a good sign,' said Jacob. 'You'll have a long happy life. If it's the herons you want to see, walk two miles till you come to the sea valley they call Volwick.'

Janet Olafson come to the door, and invited her in for a cup of tea. 'It's so hot,' said the girl, 'what I'd like most is a cup of buttermilk.'

She drank her cup of buttermilk and set out over the hill towards Volwick where the herons were.

Sometimes she stayed in the hinterland till it was dark. 'Oh,' she cried to a farmer in his lighted barn, 'I'm very happy today – I've seen a hen harrier.'

'That lass is not right in the head,' said Willie Simpson the farmer of Hillsetter to his horse . . .

There was a small croft in the barren hinterland of the island called Swinhurst. It was kept by an old woman who had only a few hens and a sheep and a goat. Winnie Swona's granddaughter – a girl of fourteen – took sick. The old woman refused to send for Dr Lamond – indeed, told the good man sharply to go about his own business when he called to see young Eliza . . . The Norday women shook their heads. The poor young lass was 'in a decline', consumption. She would be dead before harvest, little doubt of it . . . Bella Simpson of Hillsetter went so far as to peer through the window of Swinhurst after nightfall – all she could make out was the old woman sitting beside the paraffin lamp reading, and the dim shape on the bed. Then the old dog of Swinhurst got up and barked, and Bella took herself off.

115

A surer more stricken death-bed she had never seen.

The girl from the Manse called at Swinhurst with a load of daffodils in her arms. The door was opened to her by Winnie Swona at once. The girl stayed for most of the morning, in the death-house, and when she left she and the old woman stood for a while in the door, laughing – a very unseemly thing, surely, in the circumstances.

Bella Simpson looked in through the window that night. There beside poor Eliza's bed the jug of daffodils glimmered as if dew of starlight lay in every blossom.

Two mornings later Eliza was milking the goat at the end of the croft, and the very next afternoon she was turning over the earth in the planticru before the putting in and planting of the cabbage and tatties.

'Consumption!' cried Winnie Swona at the grocery van on Friday morning. 'Who said the lass had consumption? This island's full of liars. She had a bit of a spring cough, poor Eliza, that's all . . .'

And there, on the verge of spring, stood the death-bound girl dusting cobwebs from the tusker, to be ready for the peat-cutting in May.

Once the stranger met a boy who was sitting on the roadside with his schoolbag.

'The school bell went an hour ago,' she said.

'I've been sent home,' said the boy, 'for laziness and inattention. Mr Simon says I'm no good to the school or myself or the island or anybody.'

'Well done,' she said, 'you'll go places. I think you'll be a poet when you grow up. You'll be poor, of course, but you'll be a poet. How would you like that?'

The boy said he would never be good at anything. Mr Simon was very clever, he knew things. He said the boy would be a lazy idle waster all his life long.

116

The minister's guest let the boy look through her binoculars at an owl on a fencing post a mile away. Then he turned the prisms on a farm on the distant ridge. 'That's my father's farm,' he said. 'It's called Ingle. I can see my sister Sigrid feeding the hens. They're magic spy-glasses.'

As the young lady was leaving, he said, 'My name is Thorfinn Ragnarson, the idle lazy loafer.'

'I'll come and visit you in Ingle some day,' she said.

That morning Thorfinn Ragnarson was glad he had been sent home from school in disgrace.

'She's bound to get a letter one of these days,' said Isa Estquoy the postmistress-shopkeeper. 'Then we'll know her name for sure.'

But there was never any letter for the mysterious one, all the time she stayed at the Manse.

What was most surprising of all, she never turned up at the church on Sunday morning. Well, one Sunday's absence might have been excusable, but three non-attendances at the Sabbath diet of worship was astonishing – outrageous even. To be living up at the Manse and never put in an attendance Sunday after Sunday.

Revd Hector Drummond seemed quite unperturbed.

'We trust your young visitor is all right,' said Millie Smith and Bella Simpson and Thomasina Ayre in the kirk door. 'We didn't see her again in the church this morning. Of course, if she's an Episcopalian . . .'

The minister said his visitor was well and happy. No, he didn't think she was an Episcopalian, or a Roman Catholic, or a Methodist, or an agnostic. He wasn't quite sure what she was, he had never asked her. He was pretty

117

sure she had been born a Presbyterian, like them all (except Mr Harcourt-Smithers).

'Your cousin is very pretty,' said Tina Lyde.

'But she isn't my cousin, alas,' said Revd Hector Drummond.

'I didn't quite catch her name,' said Madeline Seatter.

The minister excused himself and turned to greet Jimmo the beachcomber, who hadn't been to church – the women said – since he was a peedie boy. What had drawn the ragged sea-smelling man to the kirk at last? The minister shook Jimmo's hand warmly. Jimmo had made an attempt to wash his face, he was wearing the once-posh bowler he had picked out of the ebb one old winter. He was looking a bit downcast. (Of course he had come to see the girl who had drunk tea with him on the shore one day.)

But on the following two Sundays, there was the stranger sitting in the pew immediately to the right of the pulpit. On Easter Sunday all the plain kirk windows were full of flowers. That had never happened before.

The girl in her wanderings over the islands must have met Mr Harcourt-Smithers. The next thing the village women at the well saw was someone riding the colt Selkie across the hill, and riding recklessly too, leaping over the old turf dykes and splashing through the burn. They saw, as the horse trotted down towards the village along the peat track, that it was the girl, the minister's guest. She spurred on Selkie between the beach and the village, her hair streaming out on the wind, and their onset through the village sent Billy Holm the odd-job man at the inn scurrying across the road with the cask of beer he was wheeling up from the *Raven*. The cask stottered perilously on the barrow. If it had fallen on the road and smashed a stave, there would have been a dry weekend at MacTavish's place! MacTavish shouted after the horsewoman. 'I'll report you for this, you slut, you silly idle bissom . . .' The girl's laughter sounded from the end of the village . . . The hoof echoes were suddenly muted, as horse and rider left the road and trotted beside the waves.

Nearly every morning the girl and the horse were somewhere in the island, riding along the cliffs under the screaming wheeling seabirds, along the farm roads (the working horses looked on sturdily as the stranger leaned along the neck of this lithe aristocratic horse, urging it up the hill). But mostly it was along the curving beach of coral sand that they trotted, sometimes splashing into the sea as the leisurely waves gathered and broke, coldly seething, about the horse's hooves. The girl from time to time would turn its head towards the open ocean. There the tide-rush of Norday Sound meshed with the Atlantic, in a tumult of crested waves and bell-sounds. Far out, on the horizon, a coaster would steam, Shetland-bound maybe, or a big cargo-ship between the Baltic and the Americas, deeply freighted. The girl would rise in the stirrups if a fishing boat cleared the headland, making for the village. Her call came then, cold and sweet, across the waters. And the fisherman, pursued by a rising and falling drove of gulls, would wave his arms to the sea-girl, the gutting-knife flashing in the sun.

Once, Amos Smith in the *Willa May* saw her swimming in the sea, while the horse waited patiently beside the cave . . . Amos wanted to shout a warning, that she might get caught in a tide-rip and be dragged out into the ocean, like a fish taken in a net; and there would be no help, the waters would cover her . . . But in the end Amos said

119

nothing, he watched the little splashes her arms made, and the seabattered gold of her hair.

She was surrounded, at the edge of the village, by a horde of yelling scholars, released from their prison-house at four o'clock. She leaned from the saddle as Thorfinn Ragnarson approached. 'Have you begun the poem yet, boy?' she said seriously.

The boys and girls laughed all around. The very idea, Thorfinn of Ingle writing poetry!

Thorfinn gave her a dark look – he had had trouble enough inside the school that day, without being made a fool of at the school gate! – and he ran off home across the fields.

Mr Simon was suddenly there, in the open door of the school house. 'You're very welcome,' he said. 'Come in and have a cup of coffee.'

The girl turned the horse's head without a word and rode off towards the Manse.

But there was no doubt about it, she was a well-handed girl, she wasn't a lazy idle slut at all.

How those half-dozen dingy windows of the Manse shone, after she had been at them for a week with bucket and clouts. And the neglected garden: she found a heap of empty sacks in an outhouse and she filled them to bursting with weeds from the Manse garden. She gave the rose-bushes and the gooseberry bushes room to breathe, and she pruned the old tree that had looked too wretched with time ever to leaf again; and there, in the last week of April, it unfolded morsels of greenery. The grass came, in green fresh shallows, and the daisies rushed out like stars, suddenly, and the dandelions smouldered under the wall like little shaggy suns. A bumble-bee blundered here and there, white butterflies and blue butterflies drifted among the branches. Suddenly, one morning, a blackbird began to sing on the garden wall, so that Hector Drummond paused between one bite of toast and marmalade and the next. 'Well I never,' he said to his visitor, who was pouring cups of tea. 'That blackbird's been away for a while . . . The way he goes at it! Listen . . . Spring is coming, after all. I'd quite forgotten about spring . . . Just you listen to that, you tea-wife. Song after song, stabbing the dead spirit awake . . . Oh, listen.'

'It's only a blackbird,' said the girl. 'Of course it's springtime.'

The minister drank his tea and wandered out into April. The blackbird was silent now. The dew lay on the new grass like globes of heavy crystal.

'Easter was last Sunday,' said Mr Drummond to his transfigured garden.

There was a very old ruin on the side of the hill, neglected but for an occasional amateur archaeologist.

The ruin seemed to have some religious root; the remains of a round arched window could be seen, and two indecipherable tombstones were sunk in the floor. (In summer the place was lost in nettles, thistles, hogweed.)

The shepherd Will Simpson was going home late one evening, under the first star, from seeing to a weakling lamb, when he thought he saw a glimmer among the broken walls. Occasionally a tramp visited the island, and slept under a dyke or in a cave in summer. Will Simpson thought he should look in.

It was a windless night. The lappings of ebb on shore, the hush in the shallows, the distant Atlantic sonorities, rounded out the silence. The sun was down, every hollow was brimming now with shadows. The light in the ruin shone like a ruby.

William looked carefully inside. A candle was burning in a niche. A shadow stood in the near corner, turned away, folded in silence.

A new sound came from the sea, like a struck harp. The ebb-tide had reached its mark, some time ago, and made a pause. And now, with this harp stroke, the flood-tide was beginning.

'That droll lass, the one that lives in the Manse,' said Will Simpson at the pub fire later, 'she was in that ruckle o' stones, all alone, with a star and a candle.'

The sooner she goes,' said MacTavish, 'the better it'll be. There's something unchancy about her. That one has an unsettling effect on the whole island.'

Thorfinn Ragnarson had seen from the gable-end of Ingle the light in the chapel too. He was out looking for Blip the cat. The ruin, half a mile off, had a glow-worm glimmer.

Thorfinn Ragnarson at once began on a wordless story about smugglers and casks of red wine and a little brass-bound box full of gold escudos . . . He would finish the story – wherever it was to lead him – with his head on the pillow.

*　　*　　*

One Saturday morning in May the *Raven* lay off-shore. The ship's boat had delivered a cask of beer and cases of spirits to the inn, and sacks and boxes of groceries to Isa Estquoy's shop. In the afternoon she would unload several tons of best English coal at Thomas Vass's store.

There were no passengers. The island was rarely visited,

except in high summer, when a few ornithologists and archaeologists from the south might come, or an organized picnic party from Kirkwall or Hamnavoe, or an elderly American couple seeking their roots in the parish register.

The coal was all ashore by mid-afternoon; it lay humped, a blue-black mountain, in Vass's store. The crew of the *Raven*, like black clowns with white-ringed eyes, were washing coal-dust out of their throats in MacTavish's, when Thomas Vass's Ford came stuttering and snorting down the hill road and on to the pier. Out stepped the laird, and the minister, and Thomas Vass dragged two heavy suitcases out of the boot.

Surely it was too soon for Mr Harcourt-Smithers to leave the island. In former years he would go away to shoot grouse on the twelfth of August, in the Grampians, but lately he had lingered on in his big house until the first chill of autumn.

Mr Harcourt-Smithers and Mr Drummond spoke in subdued but friendly voices. (Hitherto there had always been a kind of coldness between the laird and the minister – though traditionally they were the only two 'persons of quality' in the island and lived in the two big houses – the matter of religious adherence had tended to keep them at arms' distance.) Yet these past few weeks Mr Harcourt-Smithers and Revd Hector Drummond had been on friendly enough terms, it seemed, and had been observed calling on each other.

Matthew Ragnarson came down the pier with his son Thorfinn. The farmer of Ingle was expecting some horse-gear from the saddlery in Kirkwall.

Was it the minister who was leaving on the *Raven* that afternoon? Of course there was the General Assembly in

123

Edinburgh sometime in May, but Mr Drummond had made no announcement from the pulpit that he intended going. (But of course that meant nothing, there were such gaps and lapses in his mind.) But even if he was going to the General Assembly of the Church of Scotland for a few days, why would he be taking those two heavy cases? . . .

The chorus of Norday women gathered, one by one, at the head of the pier, and speculated and commented – only loud enough for themselves to hear.

Then the whole village heard it, the broken rhythm of hooves on the hill road, the steady beat on the tarmaced public road, and finally Selkie's hooves slackened to a walk at the end of the village. At the top of the slipway the girl dismounted. Selkie threw his head about like a wave of the sea and a little spume went on the wind. It seemed the horse was grieving. The girl put her arms about the tremulous glossy neck, and spilled the brightness of her hair over the horse's flank. And the eye of the horse rolled in his head, whether in joy or sorrow it was hard to say.

The girl gave the reins into Thomas Vass's hands. 'Thank you,' she said to the laird. 'Look after him well.'

The old man was beyond speech. He blew his nose violently into a huge red handkerchief. He went so far as to take the girl's hand and lift it almost – but not quite – to his mouth. Then he turned away abruptly and looked over the sea.

A low undersong of excitement went through the chorus of Norday women.

Men came out of the inn with mugs of beer in their hands, ploughmen and fishermen and the crew of the *Raven* with white-circled eyes in their coal-black faces.

'A good riddance, the slut,' said MacTavish.

Revd Hector Drummond had taken out his notebook and was writing in it with a stump of pencil, a thing he frequently did in his perambulations. Whether the notes were natural observations, or a sudden inspired thought, or felicitous phrases for next Sunday's sermon, only Mr Drummond knew. Today his pencil fairly scurried over the pages.

Jeph Simpson, the master of the *Raven*, cried from the deck-house, 'Put down them pints and get back to the ship. Weeds! Layabouts! We sail in ten minutes . . .' He blew on his whistle.

The throats of the coal-black drinkers convulsed as they threw back the last of their beer. 'Poor thin trash,' said the engineer. They began to drift from the pub towards the ship's boat.

The girl said to Thorfinn Ragnarson, 'You, poet, wait for me. I'll come back some day. Never forget.'

Then she actually kissed Thorfinn – a thing that had never happened before, an outrage, a public humiliation. And yet a throb of delight went through him . . . He turned away. He shook his head fiercely. His face shone with joy.

The minister put notebook and pencil in his pocket.

'Goodbye,' he said. 'Now I'll get some peace in the house.'

She kissed the minister lightly; then the red trembling cheek of the laird; then the grieving trembling face of Selkie the colt. She kissed the coal-black face of the sailor-docker who was humping her two heavy cases into the ship's boat: there was a small white dove-mark on the dark mask of his cheek.

Stepping into the small boat, she turned and blew kisses back over the island.

125

Then they rowed her out to the *Raven*. The ship got up steam. She raised anchor. She slowly backed and turned from the island and sailed off through the Sound.

Surge after surge of happiness went through Thorfinn Ragnarson.

'Blast!' said Thomas Vass. 'What way am I to get this horse and this motor-car back to the big house at the same time?'

Happiness had made the boy more bold than he had ever been. He tugged the minister by the sleeve. 'That girl,' he said, 'what's her name? I want to know.'

'Speak more respectful to Mr Drummond,' said Matthew Ragnarson sternly.

'What?' said the minister. 'What's that? Who are you, now? Oh, I've seen you before. Thorfinn – I knew it, of course – it was on the tip of my tongue . . . You want to know her name? What name? Oh, that young harridan who's been giving me no peace for a month up at the Manse. Do this, do that – eat up all your good soup – you need a new fireside rug. All that kind of interfering . . . I'm telling you, Thorfinn, I got a bit fed up of it in the end . . . Didn't you know Sophie is my young sister – well, my half-sister – my mother was a widow and married again, you see, when I was in my first year at divinity college. She said and did the strangest things, our mother . . . I think both Sophie and I are tainted – blessed is the right word for it – with her eccentricities . . . She came from the West Highlands, our mother, a bit of Gaelic enchantment in her . . . Goodness gracious, I thought everyone knew the girl's name is Sophie . . . I'm sure I let it be known . . . A dear disturbing creature . . . Sophie, that's my sister's name, but if you ask me she should have been called Persephone, it always seems to be springtime where she is . . .'

Now the *Raven* was just a wisp of smoke off Selskay island.

'Look here, Drummond,' said Mr Harcourt-Smithers, his nose redder than ever with snorting into his bandana handkerchief, 'why don't we go up to the inn and have a bite of lunch eh?'

'A good idea,' said the minister.

'What am I supposed to do with this horse?' said Vass.

'Do anything you like with it,' said the laird. 'Shoot it. Sell it. No good to me. I won't be here when the girl comes back.'

At that Selkie reared up and sent a whinny out over the sea, so poignant that even Amos Smith heard it, hauling his creels a mile away under the cliff.

'I'll take Selkie,' said Thorfinn (though he couldn't have bought a tame rabbit).

'Give the creature to that boy,' said Mr Harcourt-Smithers to his factor.

And so Thorfinn rode the horse of Persephone to Ingle and the stable and the hill.

The Press-Gang
and The Seal Dance

SOON WE MUST finish this tale of Thorfinn Ragnarson. His dreamtime is all but over, and when a child begins to think that his imaginings, his weaving of stories, are idleness, then everything about him is touched by the light of common day – that is, by the cold finger of time and mortality.

But sometimes the 'forefending angel warder' sees the child and his images through the gray bleak time of adolescence, and guides him – all unaware of such a strong anxious provident eternal friend – out into the vale of soul-making, where dream and vision are still the master-light of all his seeing. May it be so with Thorfinn Ragnarson. There are still a few incidents that may be of interest, before his story ends.

But why time should be devoted to such an unsatisfactory person, 'the idle useless boy', nobody would have been able to say then. The great English sage of the eighteenth century declared that every man has a book in him – I take that to mean that every man's life-story is a unique event, a meaningful strand in the immense unfolding web of mankind. I think it must be so, if we could view every person's life 'sub specie aeternitatis', through the eye of the guardian heaven-appointed angel. The truth is, that while we are closed in by this muddy vesture of decay, the lives of very many people, including ourselves, seem vain and futile and fleeting at last. We cling avidly, and often with despair, to the dust that is ourselves, knowing how soon it is to scatter to the twelve winds, and yet we seek to garnish this 'crudded milk, fantastical puff-paste' that is our body with as much gear and goods and gold as it can bear, and even with more than is good for it. 'We bear our heavy burden for a while, then death unloads us' . . . It is all meaningless, unless we predicate another self, a *real* self, a soul, that is seeking life-long for a true treasure, the grail . . . The trouble is, this pilgrim is hidden most of the time, only glimpsed now and again at moments of great distress or joy.

The body laments, the body dances; from somewhere deep within, in the heart's heart, or from beyond the furthest star, the good angel, the guardian, is playing on his pipe.

The music goes on and on, unheard for the most part. Through this lifetime of vanity we creep, stumble, march, follow plough and scythe, linger, hirple on a stick, until at last the feet are folded and lie still: but, seen through the angel's eye, it is an immortal spirit that dances from birth to death, all the way, from before the beginning till after the end.

Every dance, every lifetime, is unique, and that infinity of dances from every race and from every era, is of incalculable value, and comprehends the great ceremonial dance of mankind. But the music will not be known in all its glory until it is rounded with silence.

So it has been thought by some, and so I in part believe, on those rare occasions when the burden of the mystery is lifted a little.

What more must be said then about this stumbler into time – this dancer – Thorfinn Ragnarson?

*   *   *

The boy did not seem to improve with the years.

When he was fourteen he left school, to his own relief and to a curt dismissal from Mr Simon.

He helped his father on the croft of Ingle for a year or two. Neither father nor son was a notable agriculturist – no trophies were brought home to Ingle for the prize cow or the prize pig at the agricultural show in August. The cornland of Ingle seemed always a bit more scraggy and thin than the surging green and gold of the summer corn at Simon Taing's Bu farm, or at the Glebe, or Updike.

Inga, Thorfinn's eldest sister, got married to quite a prosperous farmer in the neighbouring island of Selskay, and that wedding – which had of necessity to be in the barn of the bride's home – left Matthew Ragnarson a little in debt. (But Matthew wasn't foolish enough to make too big a splash.)

Then Sigrid, the second daughter, left to work in a grocer's shop in Kirkwall, and soon met a boy there, and there was another marriage, though not in the barn of Ingle. The reception was in a hired hall in Kirkwall, to Matthew Ragnarson's relief, though he did regret a little this breaking of an old tradition. The wedding guests danced to guitars and accordions – a South-born caterer supplied the tasteless food – funny telegrams were read.

He put on his black Sunday suit and went to the wedding, and gave his daughter an envelope with a ten-pound note in it, and was home on the *Raven* next morning.

Tina Lyde was often at the door of Ingle, sometimes with jars of rhubarb jam, or with a segment of the cheese she made herself, or with a thick woollen jersey in October, so that the farmer of Ingle would endure the winter without colds or pleurisy . . . One day Tina Lyde arrived with a gift of a rag mat to lay on the flagstone floor of Ingle, beside the hearth. That day, Tina came in without knocking. Ragna, who was a gentle girl, said her father wasn't at home – he had gone to see Albert Laird the joiner about a new cattle stall for the byre. Ragna said they didn't really want a mat on the floor, there was a danger of fire, a live coal might topple from the stacked smouldering peats. Tina Lyde spread the rag mat on the floor: it looked well enough, it seemed to brighten the room with its well-chosen dapplings of green and blue, like the colours of Norday itself. Ragna stooped and rolled up the mat and thrust it into Tina Lyde's arms. 'Take it away from here!' Ragna shouted. 'We want none of your charity. Leave our father alone. I'd be glad if you never darkened this door again.'

Thorfinn could hear his sister's voice from the hayfield.

Then he saw Tina Lyde walking back to the village, rapidly, shaking her head vehemently as she went.

When Thorfinn went inside, he found Ragna in a storm of tears. It was unusual – the anger and the weeping – from a placid girl like Ragna.

Thorfinn closed the door softly and went back to the hayfield, and picked up his scythe.

That summer the farms of Glebe and Bu and Westvoe got tractors, and their horses were sold at the Kirkwall mart. The tractors mowed down the hayfields swiftly and efficiently.

Tina Lyde didn't come back to Ingle again with gifts. Matthew Ragnarson wondered why, aloud one night over supper. 'Tina hasn't been here for a week or two,' he said. 'I'm partial to her oatcakes and rhubarb jam.'

Ragna and Thorfinn looked at each other, and were silent.

Tina never came back to Ingle with gifts. But that summer, in the lingering twilight of evening, Ragna or Thorfinn might glimpse her on the hillside above the farm or on the shore below, looking towards Ingle. The shadows thickened about her. Sunset and dawn mingled their fires. When Thorfinn went out, at midnight, to see that the meadow gate was secure, there sometimes the woman was still, under the few stars of summer.

*   *   *

The wheel of time went round, in Norday more slowly it seemed than in other places, but it brought changes.

One day the farmer of Ingle came home from the village with a large box in his cart. He carried it inside and set it on the table. It was a wireless set, and it required fairly complicated adjustments by Ben Hoy, who was knowledgeable about electrical things – having knocked about the seaports of the world for years – the rigging of an aerial, the attachment of a wet battery, an earth-wire. Then the switching-on, and the music of Henry Hall and the BBC Dance Orchestra, and later at night such blood-curdling dramas as *Murder in the Red Barn*, and Scottish dance music – and one night they heard a voice screaming and ranting and raging in a foreign language . . . Ragna couldn't stand it any more; she rose and switched the wireless off. (At that voice even the dog Stalwart lay whining on the floor.) They found out later that it was the ruler of Germany, Adolf Hitler, saying that his patience was exhausted, that his claim to Sudetenland was the last territorial demand he had to make in Europe . . . Oh, it was a hideous voice, Ragna said it frightened her more – far more – than *Murder in the Red Barn* . . .

Mr Harcourt-Smithers sent word to his factor Thomas Vass that he wouldn't be coming to Norday this summer. Perhaps next summer, if his health improved.

Revd Hector Drummond announced from his pulpit one Sunday that he had received a call from a congregation in Coatbridge, Lanarkshire. He thanked his parishioners for their great patience and kindness over the past years – how many? – five? six? . . . Oh, it didn't matter, such goodness was hoarded in eternity . . . He felt he had been in many ways an unworthy pastor . . . But he loved them dearly, each and every one of them, whether they had attended the kirk or not . . . In Coatbridge he would often think of the folk of this island – what was its name again? – this wayward mind of his! – oh, indeed, Norday . . . How could he ever have forgotten it for the fraction of a moment – it was graven in his heart.

Many in the congregation felt sorrow at the imminent departure of Mr Drummond, none more so than the heir to Ingle croft. Now the girl Sophie would never come to Norday again . . . He gave the horse Selkie a feed of best oats that evening.

Three very important-looking men arrived on the *Raven* one day in the summer of 1937, just after Norday had celebrated the coronation of King George VI and Queen

134

Elizabeth with a fire on the top of the hill Fea, and sports in the big field behind the school. The inn did a roaring trade, and Isa Estquoy had set up a tea tent on the sports ground. Nobody knew how many sandwiches were eaten that day, or cakes, or bars of Cadbury's, Fry's and Rowntree's chocolate. The field at last light was littered with empty lemonade bottles, chocolate wrappings, swee-tie bags, and cigarette packets.

It was to an island satiated with festival that the three mysterious strangers came. In those days, the country people went out of their way to be pleasant and welcoming to visitors, but those men, from first setting foot on Norday, didn't seem to care what the islanders thought of them. They climbed through fences and trespassed on fields; they even walked through the young green corn of the Glebe and the Bu. Simon Taing of the Bu came out and remarked that the gentlemen were in his barleyfield. They looked at the farmer coldly, and made some measurements and set up a tripod, right there in the middle of the barley, and looked in all directions through some kind of an instrument, and one of them spoke some numbers, and another made notes in a large notebook. Lucky, the Bu collie, didn't like the look of them, it seemed, for he went circling behind the man with the theodolite and suddenly made a grab at the man's trouser-leg. 'Keep that brute under control,' the man taking notes said . . . Simon Taing called in the dog, and said that Lucky had never been known to seize anyone before – all the same, it was his land they were trespassing on, his barley, the winter bread of the people, and he would be glad to know what they were there for, anyway . . . The three men paid no attention to the farmer. They viewed, chanted numbers, made notes. Then they checked

135

everything carefully, their heads all together, and folded up their gear, and climbed through the barbed wire into Glebe farm and began to perform the same ritual there . . . There was a cluster of fertile farms on this level part of the island.

At the Glebe, John Kerrigan was too bashful to go out and have words with the mysterious men. But Matilda his wife went out, wiping her fingers on her dish-towel. 'Won't you come in for a cup of tea?' she asked. 'You're welcome.'

The men were setting up their tripod in the big field of greening oats. They paid Matilda Kerrigan no more attention than if she had been a shrilling seagull. They didn't so much as look at her.

'Are you from the Ministry of Agriculture and Fisheries?' said Matilda. 'They usually send a letter saying they're coming, and they're very nice men when they do come. I can tell you this, we're not claiming subsidies we're not entitled to.'

The setting of the instrument on the tripod here and there, this way and that, the tilting and adjusting, viewing, the litany of numbers, the note-taking, the consultation, the nodding of heads, the feet in the young oats.

It was more than Mrs Matilda Kerrigan could bear. She was what they called in Norday 'a hasty woman' – generous, impulsive, quick to take umbrage. She ran at the intruders and kicked the tripod, and the instrument fell on the green braird with a clatter. Fortunately the earth was soft with rain and wind and sun, and with the subtle irreversible upthrust of the young oats; so the three, after a quick panicky examination, decided that their instrument wasn't at all damaged. 'But,' said the man with the notebook, 'you, madam, will be hearing about this.

You could go to prison for a very long time, for what you've done. No, I don't want to know your name. We know your name. We know the names of everyone in this island. I advise you to go indoors and not show yourself, till we've done our work . . .' '*You'll* hear about it too,' cried Matilda. 'The like of this has never happened in this island before. We have lawyers in Kirkwall, yes and a county councillor and an MP. You're the ones who'll soon be in severe trouble!'

John Kerrigan stood in the farm house door, pleading with his wife Matilda to shut her mouth and come indoors before she got them into deep trouble.

'The trash!' cried Matilda.

Courtesy or insults, it was all the same to them. They carried on in the oatfield of Glebe until their work was done. Then they climbed over the barbed wire fence and set up their instrument in the fallow land of Ingle . . .

In all, they visited six farms and crofts in the lowlands of Norday that morning, including Ingle. They had a quick lunch at the inn and left at three o'clock on the *Raven*. And that, for a while, was that. Nothing seemed to follow from the events of that morning. It remained a mystery, for a full year almost.

At Ingle, one morning just before harvest, Matthew Ragnarson came in to his dinner of broth and beef and tatties, apple dumpling, and a mug of tea. He didn't eat as heartily as usual, and whenever Thorfinn and Ragna spoke to him, he mumbled and seemed to look anywhere but into their eyes – a strange thing in a man so simple and straightforward.

'Are thu no weel, daddo?' said Ragna anxiously.

Nothing ailed him, said the farmer of Ingle. Yet the

137

colour came and went in his face, and he cleared his throat once or twice as if he wanted to speak and yet was having difficulty in putting the words in order. 'I'm all right in my health,' he said . . . Then he looked at them across the table, and a deeper flush came on his face, and he said in a distinct but unnatural voice, 'I have something to tell you. Ragna and Thorfinn, I am to be married again. I have been a lonely man since your mother died. I could bear it, when you were all bairns. Now you've grown up, and two of you aren't here at Ingle any more, and you, Ragna, I know you've been meeting Andrew Rosey the ferryman, and it won't be long till you're married and settled in the boathouse. The boy and I, we'll be needing somebody to run this house.'

Ragna said nothing. Thorfinn went on eating his Eve's pudding, but he dug his spoon in more slowly, and he gave his father one look only, as if the man at the head of the table was an utter stranger, and a rather unwelcome one.

'I am not courting Andrew Rosey,' said Ragna in a voice like lead. 'I am not going to be Andrew Rosey's wife . . .' Then she rose to her feet and shrilled at her father, 'What an insult to our mother, taking a woman like that into our house! Think shame of yourself. A tittle-tattle and a mischief-maker!'

Thorfinn had never seen his sister so wrought up. The white mask of her face frightened him. 'Now now,' was all he could stammer. 'Please, Ragna.' But he felt coldness and emptiness there where his heart normally beat in a dreamy contented rhythm.

The dog Stalwart sniffed at Matthew Ragnarson's taut fingers, and whined and showed the whites of his eyes, and went out into the yard and the sunlight.

The rage went out of Ragna's voice. She looked at her father affectionately and sadly. 'Have I not looked after you well enough here? Didn't you get three good meals in the day, and a fire to come home to, and thick clothes to wear in winter? Wasn't I here to welcome anyone that came to the door, whether it was Jimmo Greenay come begging, or Vass the factor, the postman or the rat-catcher, everybody? Surely the butter here at Ingle is as good as any farm-wife's butter, and the rhubarb jam as tart in the mouth . . . Oh daddo, could you endure to have another hand turning my mother's spinning wheel, and emptying the big heavy crumbly cheeses out of her cheese-mould? It seems like a defilement, that that woman should so much as turn a chair or lift the poker to stir the fire – all the things touched by our mother are good and beautiful to me . . . Still, man, I wish you well . . . I think I've never said this before, but I love you dearly . . . And I'm not going to marry into the boat-house. But neither am I going to stay in this house with that woman . . .'

Matthew Ragnarson tried to take his daughter's hand as she went quickly past him out through the door of Ingle into the sunlight. But she shook his hand from her.

There was no more dinner at Ingle that day.

Matthew Ragnarson went and stood in the very darkest corner of the room, his face turned away from the sun-smitten door and the red and gray of the fire.

Thorfinn went out to the field and spoke for an hour and more to Selkie the horse; then he mounted Selkie and they rode up the peat track to the summit of Fea . . . The island lay below them, the greens of meadow and pasture, the bronze of harvest in a dozen fields, surging in the wind; a fisherman at the slipway with baskets of haddock (Amos Smith), two more fishing boats in the open Sound with flickers of gulls behind; the *Raven* steaming slow between Selskay and Njalsay islands.

It seemed, from so high up, to be an idyll of peace and absolute security.

The cows moved as if tranced through the clover fields. From far away, dogs barked.

A farm-worker here and there went between barn and barleyfield.

The only gloomy place in Norday was the great Hall; it seemed to Thorfinn that no one would ever live there again.

Outside the inn, Howie Ayre and Geordie Wylie sat on a bench and drank their beer, and smoked . . . They must have been saying droll things to Bella Simpson who was standing with her zinc bucket at the well, for she stopped and set down the bucket – that blazed with the sun, once – and put her hands to her huge hips and threw back her head in outraged merriment. The thin echo of Bella Simpson's voice came fragile to the top of Fea, *So Tina's got him at last. . . Nothing like persistence . . .*

From the school drifted the thin chant of the Norday children reciting multiplication tables.

Thorfinn looked everywhere to find his sister – he could not mistake Ragna, the flow and rhythm of her movements. Nothing – his sister was nowhere to be seen in all the island . . . He thought at once – the melancholy dreamer that he was – of suicide: a betrayed abandoned girl hurling herself off the cliff into the sea below.

But he knew that that was impossible, with Ragna.

It was warm up here on the summit of Fea. Thorfinn let Selkie wander among the scree and heather. He set his back against a sun-warmed rock.

A hill croft here and there had been abandoned, and was slowly tumbling into ruin. Janet Olafson had recently died in Smylder, and already starlings were flying in and out of a broken pane . . . The month before she died Janet Olafson had met Thorfinn on the road. 'Boy,' she had said, 'I want you to know this – old Jacob said you were to have his fishing boat the *Scallop*. Yes, it's all down in black and white . . .' So far, Thorfinn had received no notification: as far as he knew, that fishing boat was slowly rotting down at the noust, like Smylder itself . . .

But the poorest croft in the island, Swinhurst, still had its hens, its cat, and its goat and few sheep. Thorfinn could see, that very minute, Eliza Swona milking the goat beside the well.

How sad this day had been! He had tasted love, in the spring, one enchanting sip – it must surely be a state of inexpressible joy! Yet here, today, in this island – in the croft house of Ingle – love had turned out to be a cruel and twisted and sad business. He had not known, in Ingle, a more distressful day – not even his mother's death; he had been too young to know much about that.

Selkie had found a patch of grass among the heather and scree, and was lingering there, cropping.

Another waking dream fell about the boy, as the lark mounted higher and higher on his blue ladder of song, as the kestrel slouched about the hill, not far below the boy's feet, and paused, and fell like a stone into a hidden hollow.

*   *   *

It was the reign of good King George III.

In Norday they knew nothing of war, unless a Dutch ship off-shore brought news, in broken English, that the

141

British and the French were at their everlasting wars again. It was all one to them. The Dutch skipper – a smuggler – might as well have told them that the Faroese were at their whale-culling, or the Icelandic volcano was active again. Wars were in the nature of things, but happened otherwise.

But one summer the laird had ridden down, he had visited every croft in the island (in those days the laird owned every grain of earth, every salt crystal, in Norday). 'The king is at war with the French,' he said. 'Not the French king, there is no French king any more. The French rabble have risen against their king and queen and cut off their heads, as well as the heads of all the aristocrats, the hereditary guardians of the poor and defence-less.' (He was going to add that he too was their guardian, but thought better of it, for this particular laird – John Smithers Esquire, of Norday in the county of Orkney, Member of Parliament – unlike his father and grandfather, was a hard man and wrung every last drop of sweat from the enforced labourers in his big harvest field, as well as the increased rents he had burdened them with – and he saw too, at nearly every door, the stubborn looks and the contemptuous looks and the frightened looks they gave him.) 'King George,' he went on, 'is building a great fleet of warships to fight against the French rebels and regicides. Many seamen will be needed to man those ships from all over the kingdom.' (This, the islanders knew, was a lie – the Dutch skipper, and other visiting skippers besides, had told how the recruiting officers, otherwise known as the press-gang, were having a hard job finding volunteers in every seaport in the land, and so they were scouring the waterfront, gathering into their net all the jailbirds and drunks and innocents they could take, and

142

those were the hearts-of-oak and the heroes who were to fight the dastardly French on the sea.) 'So now,' went on the young laird, 'the time has come for the young men in this remote part of the kingdom to do their duty. I know all the young men of Norday will be only too eager to volunteer. When His Majesty's recruiting officers arrive soon, I expect a full muster of men in the courtyard of the Hall, ready and willing to take the king's shilling. Think, then, what adventures will lie before you young yokels. You will see lands and seas and cities you never dreamed of – you'll see the sugar plantations of Jamaica and the teeming bazaars of Morocco, as well as the gorgeous palaces and solemn temples of London. But, above and beyond all that, you'll have done your duty and blown the ships of the king-murdering French from the face of the ocean. Now, then, can I have a name or two?'

Not a hand was raised. Sullen stubborn faces looked back at John Smithers, laird of Norday, and Member of Parliament for the northern burghs . . . At last a single hand went wavering up, but it belonged to poor Elijah Ayre, who had been a simpleton since birth.

'Not you, Elijah, alas,' said the young laird. 'You won't do, Elijah.'

A ripple of laughter went over the men of Norday, the mockery directed more at Mr Smithers than Elijah.

'Very well,' said the laird, and stooped from his horse to say a quiet word to Elphinstone his factor, who produced a rolled and ribboned scroll from inside his coat and passed it to the laird.

'Here,' said the laird, 'I have a complete list of all the young men in this island of mine, those sound in wind and limb, and I am commanded by their lordships of

Admiralty to supply suitable men to serve as seamen on board His Majesty's men-of-war . . .'

Then Mr Smithers read out a dozen names. 'The men I have just named will assemble here on Tuesday at noon. The sloop *Torbay* will be anchored in the Sound. Those volunteers will be taken by the recruiting officers on to the *Torbay*, and conveyed thence to the Nore or to Portsmouth. Make no mistake about it. This is how it must be. You should be happy and proud to serve your king and country . . . You understand, this enrolment will be a loss to me financially, in that I will lack your labour on sea and land, and must expect diminished returns in the way of rental.'

Nothing more was said.

The island men dispersed to their farms. A few of them went to the ale-house kept then by an old woman called Kitty Fea, and they drank and talked in whispers – their heads close together at the fireside table – till well after midnight.

The *Torbay* dropped anchor in the Sound on Tuesday morning, early.

The recruiting officers ('the press-gang') were met by the laird at the garden gate. Mr Smithers had to tell the sergeant that the twelve men nominated for recruitment had not turned up in the yard – not one. 'They are an obdurate and stiff-necked people,' said the laird. 'I had hoped the recruitment could have been carried out amicably on all sides. I know, sergeant, that I am ultimately responsible. Now I see that there will be certain difficulties. You have my permission to compel those men into His Majesty's service. You will find them in the usual places – in the fields, down at the fishing-boats. Elphinstone here will accompany you. Use no more force than is necessary, sergeant.'

144

But when the press-gang went in search of the young men, the twelve nominated, they were not to be found, neither in the barns nor at the boat nousts. It seemed they had vanished clean from the island. Oh no, the old folk, their parents, could offer no help. One, it seemed, had embarked on a whaling ship in Hamnavoe. One had gone to Shetland to get a wife there. One had sailed that very morning in his yole to sell two young sheep in Caithness, they did not know when their Adam would be back. One, James Laird the joiner, was in Kirkwall taking possession of a cargo of Norwegian timber; there would be coffins to be made in winter, and cradles, and bed and table and chairs for them that would be getting married after harvest – and when James went to Kirkwall for wood, said his grandmother, it was hard to know when he would be back in the island, drunk or sober . . .

It was not only the twelve on the laird's list that had left Norday on urgent business – not a single hale-and-hearty young man was to be found anywhere in the island.

One old woman, Jemima Hoy, said the peedie folk, the trows, the trolls, the fairiks, had taken them away. Such things had been known in olden times, Jemima Hoy assured Elphinstone and the sergeant. The sergeant had given her a sixpenny piece to tell them where the young men might be. Jemima Hoy laughed. Then she spat viciously at the sergeant's feet. Then she turned and went with her sixpence to Kitty Fea's ale-house.

Ah, but at the croft of Ingle it seemed they were in luck. Yes, said the croft-wife Liza Ragnarson, her son Thorfinn was at home. Very sorrowfully she said it. She would be proud and glad indeed to offer her boy Thorfinn to be a sailor of the king – nothing more wonderful could happen to the lad on the croft of Ingle, or to Norday or

to the whole of Orkney, than that her one and only son
Thorfinn should fight against the French on a man-of-war.
Alas! . . . And here the poor woman broke down, there
on the threshold of Ingle, and wept bitterly.

'You need have no fear, Mistress Ragnarson,' said
Elphinstone the factor. 'Your boy will be treated honour-
ably. The war will not last long. The French ships are
already blockaded in their ports – the cowards. When
desperation forces them out into the open sea, they will
be blown to pieces by our guns. Thorfinn will be home
again in the spring, a young man rich in experience, yes,
and in more than experience, in the bounty money that
will belong to all sailors at the war's end . . .'

The wife of Ingle continued to weep, more bitterly than
ever, and urged them over the threshold. Inside Ingle it
was gloomy, the only light came from a skylight. The air
was heavy with peatsmoke from a fire in the middle of
the room. A sow grunted among her farrow at the far
side of the hearth. The sergeant covered his mouth with
a kerchief, one of his men had to go outside to clear
the peatsmoke from his lungs. Elphinstone coughed and
hawked vigorously into the peat-glow. The factor's cough
was echoed feebly by a loose feeble choking from a box-
bed in the corner, that seemed to go on and on, and ended
in a half-strangled groan. Their eyes got accustomed to
the gloom. They saw a shape in the bed, and the young
man's head on the hempen pillow seemed to glow with
fever; he turned his face towards them, and his face was
silvered suddenly with a gush of sweat. Then the feeble
cough possessed him again, and his whole body shook and
trembled.

'Consumption,' said Mistress Ragnarson. 'He's on his
death-bed. It can't be long now.'

146

Another of the press-gang went out and was sick among the nettles of the planticru.

'Could I have a word with your man?' said Elphinstone.

'He's up with the sheep,' said the croft-wife. 'I think he's glad to be up in the wind and the sun, anywhere to be away from this sorrow that's come on us, for an hour or two.'

'Well,' said Elphinstone, 'I grieve for you, poor woman. You have other children, have you not?'

'One lass, Lizzie – she's a servant over at the Manse. The minister's wife gives Lizzie a bed in the garret. I'm glad of that, Mr Elphinstone and you other gentlemen. The consumption is very smitsom, I wouldn't wish an early grave on my lass too. This is the galloping consumption, the worst kind, it goes through a district like wildfire. Oh sirs, I've known whole families wiped out.'

The box-bed echoed with another bout of coughing. The narrow wooden cave seemed to exude a sulphurous fetor.

'Are you not feared, woman, that the trouble will grip you too?' said Elphinstone with a kind of rough kindness.

'Nothing seems to touch me,' said Mistress Ragnarson. 'The measles, the smallpox, the mumps, the Baltic fever – they've all been in Norday in my time, and not one of them came near me, though folk were dropping all about me. The whooping cough, it carried off my sister and my father, and I was there to close their eyes and make a supper three days after for the mourners . . . Ah well, so long as I can ease the last struggles of this poor boy, and cross his hands, and see him well shrouded. I should be thankful, though it's a hard thing to lose an only son. His shroud has been waiting in the kist over there since he was an infant, against the day of his death, whenever that might come. It can't be long now, sirs.'

'We'll trouble you no further then, Mistress Ragnarson,' said Elphinstone. 'You have troubles enough, the Lord knows.'

'It's good of you to call,' said the wife of Ingle. 'I'm sorry my man's up with the sheep. I wish you all success in your errand here in Norday, whatever that may be . . .'

So Elphinstone and the men of the press-gang went out into the blinding sunlight.

'Oh, mother, help me . . . I think there's more blood from my throat . . .' They turned their faces to the next croft.

Not one recruit did they take in the island that day.

In the evening they had supper with Mr Smithers at the Hall. The laird was very angry. 'It will be the worse for me,' he said, pouring out brandy for himself and the sergeant, and ale into pewter mugs for the others. 'I am ultimately responsible. I will be blamed for this failure by their lordships of Admiralty. It may be, the expenses of this day will be put on me. I can ill afford that.'

The sergeant suggested one solution – to seize a few of the older men, those over forty say, and a few boys of thirteen to fifteen years, and so make up the quota. But the laird quickly vetoed this suggestion.

Elphinstone kept to his own cottage. He was in most disgrace of all. The laird knew, and the factor knew, that the wanted men were holed up in a cave somewhere on the far side of the island, where the six-hundred-foot crags abruptly sheer up over the Atlantic. The factor ought to know everything about an island, surely. Elphinstone was not to be blamed, however, for only two or three very old men – fowlers and cragsmen in their youth – knew where the cave was, and those ancients, questioned, said they had known once but had long forgotten. This much was certain, when word of a Dutch or a French ship laden with smuggled brandy, tobacco, or tea was brought, the whole island was alerted: the barrels and boxes and chests were brought ashore in moon-dark, by the light of one feeble lantern, and what wisdom directed them to this fissure in the crag face seemed to be mysteriously there, urging and directing . . . But in the light of day, next morning, or any morning later, just where the cave was could not be known for sure, even to those islanders who had unloaded the cargo into their yoles and cobles from the foreign hold, and heaved them from hand to hand, up the cliff into the treasure hole . . .

The cave had been sanctuary in Norday for centuries . . . This was not the first time . . . In the long-ago, there had been pirates from Lewis, and predators out of Buchan and Caithness and the Lothians in the days of Earl Patrick Stewart.

'We will not be looking for thanks or promotion ourselves,' said the sergeant to the laird.

Mr Smithers poured more dollops of consolation from the crystal brandy jar.

'Dying?' he said. 'The boy Ragnarson dying? Consumption is it . . . ?' It occurred to him later that night, getting ready for bed, that he had seen young Ragnarson three days before, pushing out his yole, stacked with creels for the lobster-fishing. 'Decline, consumption, is a swift and sure killer,' he said to his young wife. 'Is it possible for the consumption to strike down a young strong man so suddenly, in the course of three days, and burn him in its fires . . . ?'

That night he remembered to say a prayer before he slept.

Next morning the officers of the press-gang sailed from Norday in the *Torbay*, back to Kirkwall.

Mr Smithers was at the beach. He bade them a somewhat contemptuous farewell.

The sergeant said he thought there was little likelihood of them returning. No one willingly sets foot on a barren island.

Elphinstone stayed indoors.

The Admiralty boat lingered out in the Sound till the wind began to fill the sails. Then she headed for Kirkwall.

The laird heard voices from the sea-banks above. He turned. The whole island seemed to be there, old people and children too. Once the sailing-boat had cleared the headland, everyone broke into cheering. A few of the girls seemed to be dancing on the links. The children laughed and clapped their hands.

Mr Smithers shaded his eyes and looked back at his people. It could not be! It was impossible, surely! There stood the twelve men nominated for enrolment in His Majesty King George III's navy, all in a laughing group – the one who had sailed for the Greenland whaling, the one who had gone to Shetland for a wife, the one who was to be a full week in Kirkwall settling his payment for the Norwegian trees, all of those taken by the trows under the hill. And there among the others stood the young man of Ingle who had been on his death-bed yesterday, in the sulphurous chokings and burnings of consumption.

The twelve young men raised such cheerings that old

John Olafson had to hush them, lest the press-gang heard the mockery, and turned back with their muskets primed and cocked.

Mr Smithers strode past them without a word, back to the Hall, where his beautiful young wife was waiting to console him.

There, where the island girls had tried out a few tentative steps and leaps an hour before, dancing went on all day till the sun went down. A barrel of ale was heaved down among the rocks by three young men. Thomas Kerrigan went home to fetch his fiddle.

But the Thorfinn Ragnarson of two centuries ago stood alone, above, among the kingcups and the thrift.

The trouble was, he was shy of girls.

Presently he turned and walked away across the wide beach, where the seals tumbled on and off the skerry. He whistled. The seals turned wondering faces towards the song.

The young man was back again, at twilight, among the dunes.

And there, on the sand, glimmering, were men and women – strangers – dancing! And the rocks were strewn with sealskins.

The seal people danced to music unheard.

There was one girl among the seal people and she was so beautiful that Thorfinn had a catch in his breath, suddenly, and he gave a low cry of longing.

The girl was not a part of the seal dance. She crouched beside the rock. How could it be, that none of the seal men wanted to dance with her?

Perhaps she heard Thorfinn's low cry, for she turned her face and looked up at the dunes. But she could not see him, hidden there, in the long thin tall grasses.

The sun was down, the light was thickening. The waves lapped higher among the stones and rockpools.

The seal people went on with their joyous interweavings and circlings and unfoldings. It was a beautiful dance to look at, but the young crofter had eyes only for the girl who, for some reason, was not permitted to dance.

The selkie ears are pure and delicate, they can hear sounds that human ears are too gross to take in. Listen! They have heard something perilous. The leader of the dance holds up his finger. The dance stops. All the ocean faces turn to the dunes and the hidden watcher. It can't be, surely, that they hear the thundering of the boy's heart, his broken breathing. The scoldings of the oyster-catcher can only mean that some creature, cat or hare or man, is too near her nest.

No, it seems all right, the dance can go on. The girl who has been left at the rock for some misdemeanour or disobedience – but how could so lovely a creature behave badly? – continues to glance, more and more often, at the sand-dune where Thorfinn lies hidden.

He can endure it no longer. The grass rustles. Thorfinn gets to his feet. There he stands against the sky, a man, and dangerous. (For what evils have men not put on the seal tribes, for generations and for centuries?)

The dance is broken! In wild confusion the seal people run towards the skins that they have left on the rocks. Quickly they draw their coats about them and tumble, one after another, into the sea . . . They drift out into the Sound, their heads shining like bottles under the first stars.

But the girl cannot join her tribe in their trek to the ocean. She is searching everywhere for her sealskin. She

looks under the swathes of seaweed. Surely she left it on
that rock studded with seven limpets. No – not there. Her
coat is lost!

A star-cast shadow falls over her. There, standing
behind her, is the stranger from the world of men. He is
gripping her sealskin in his fist.

She pleads for it, wordlessly. Let her have it, oh please
– she must go back to her people in the ocean! If she
cannot get her coat, she will perish miserably among salt-
less ruts and roots of the earth.

She reaches out, touches her coat, her fingers close on
the briny fur. The man tears the coat from her hand.

He points. He gestures inland towards the croft of
Ingle. She must follow him up the cart track.

Now she trembles, the dew shimmers slow down the
darkening air upon the grass and the crops and the wild
meadowsweet of Norday island. It is growing colder by
the minute. The stars thicken.

Thorfinn takes off his own coat and throws it over the
girl. His coat smells of corn and peats and cows, she does
not like it.

'Come,' says Thorfinn.

He seizes her, a bit roughly, by the hand, and begins
to lead her up the track to the sea-banks above.

The girl turns. She looks long out over the darkening
heave of ocean. The seal-tribe, her kin, have vanished.

She weeps awhile.

Then she follows the man up to the sea banks and
across the fields.

The man of Ingle and his wife are at their supper of oat
bannocks and cheese and ale. Two fish-oil lamps burn at
the wall, there is a glow from the banked-up peats.

Thorfinn comes in, hiding a bundle under his jersey.

'What keeps you from your supper?' says the mother. 'We'd thought the press-gang men had come back in secret and taken you to the wars, after all my schemings.'

The father says nothing. He nods. He would not for one moment have thought his Liza could be so bold and so clever, to cheat the press-gang like that. And Thorfinn, too, he had played the part of a death-bound young man to perfection. And yet there was something unchancy about it; he had said to his wife that they might all be punished for such a deception, people ought always to be plain and direct in their dealings one with another, and then in the eye of heaven they had nothing to fear. But Liza had curled her lip at her pious kirk-going man. Hadn't Jacob come into the inheritance and the blessing by a ruse, putting rabbit-fur on his hands when he brought the savoury stew to his old blind father, the patriarch Isaac, so that Isaac thought it was the hairy hands of his brother Esau the hunter that brought him supper to the tent that solemn night . . . And hadn't the brothers of Joseph brought the bloodied coat of many colours to their old father, saying that the young brother – the dreamer – must have been devoured by a lion, on his way to them carrying bread and meat from the tents – so that the old father all but died of grief, but not quite, for he lived many years after that deception – long enough indeed, to see how that deception bore within itself a great blessing, for Joseph, cast into the pit by his ox-headed brothers and sold to wandering merchants, became a great man in Egypt, the Pharaoh's chief councillor, the provider of bread for all the hungry tribes and cities of the east, and the bestower of bread and more than bread to the Israelites, his own people. And that same Joseph, had he not practised deception on the brothers, including Benjamin the innocent youngest, putting silver cups and plates into their corn-sacks, so that on the frontier when the Egyptian guards accused them falsely, the sacks were opened and there the silver glittered in the cruel sun, and a terrible fear fell on the eleven . . .

So the wife of Ingle tattled on and on, and silenced the qualms of her gentle pious husband. What was wrong with the deceiving of a band of licensed ruffians, who would have dragged their only boy, their Thorfinn, off to the guns and the drowning waters of war – a war that had nothing whatever to do with their peaceful island?

'Let be, let be,' said the father, tired of her ranting on and on – and yet well pleased that by such devious ways she had saved their son to carry on the work of the little farm in the hills.

'Draw in your chair and have a bite of supper,' says Liza to Thorfinn now.

But Thorfinn sets the ladder against a rafter and climbs up among the shadows and the hens and the spiders'-webs.

'I'll hand him up a candle to give him some light, whatever he's at,' says Liza. But the words aren't out of her mouth before Thorfinn is down again.

The mother points to the chair and the supper table.

Thorfinn hesitates. Then he says solemnly, 'I've found a lass. She's waiting outside. I'll take her in now to meet you.'

Thorfinn opens the door and bids the girl come in. She comes in, and brings with her the coldness of sea and starlight.

'Who is she?' says the croft-wife. 'What's her name? She's not an island lass, I've not seen her before. Why is she wearing your coat?'

155

'Now, now,' says the crofter, 'no need to speak so fierce and tart to her. She's frightened, the lass. Be gentle with her.'

But Liza rages at her son, louder than ever. 'Where did you find her, you fool? She's not staying here, let me make that plain. Why doesn't she say a word? She frightens me more than the press-gang. Take her back where you found her.'

Now the seal-girl holds fast to Thorfinn's hand. She is afraid of everything, the rage of the woman, the enclosing walls and the smoky thatch; she flinches from the fire and the two lamps as if she felt the scalds at the heart of them.

'I don't know who she is,' says the boy. 'I don't know where she comes from. She says her name is Mara. I'm going to marry her.'

'He could do worse, he could do worse,' says the father. 'She looks a fine enough lass to me. Come over to the table, lass, put in your hand, you're welcome to a bite of bread and cheese.'

'Either that creature goes,' says Liza in a low voice, 'or I go. I won't bide a night under the same roof with her!'

Now the father and the son pay no heed to the mother. The stranger is ushered to a chair at the table. Thorfinn puts the food and a frothing mug in front of her. And he sits opposite her, and begins to eat and drink. But the girl covers her face with her hands. She cannot taste this earth-food.

'You must eat, or you'll dwine away,' says the crofter of Ingle. 'You're most welcome . . .' Then he turns to Thorfinn and says, 'I don't know if she understands me or not, but the more I see of this lass the more I like her. I'm glad she's come to bide here. There'll be bairns in this house, and not before time. There'll be a good woman to see to the fire and the spinning-wheel and the butter-making when we old ones are dust in the kirkyard.'

At that, a moan comes from the wife of Ingle. She goes and sits, trembling, in the straw chair beside the fire, as if she feels the first shadow of death on her. Her face is gray.

Still Mara won't lift the oatcake to her lips, though Thorfinn comes to her and tells her how it must be done, first the buttering of the oatcake, then the cutting of a wedge of cheese. The girl pushes the plate away.

Now the boy presses his hand to his forehead. Of course, he ought to have known. He goes to the pail of fish, new-caught by his father that morning, in the wall niche, and brings two small haddocks and puts them on her plate . . . At once she begins to eat, slowly and tremulously at first, lowering her face to gnaw sweetly at the raw silver. But soon she uses her fingers to lift the fish to her mouth.

'Good,' says James Ragnarson. 'But I think soon you'll enjoy the lobsters and the cod better if they're simmered a while in the pot. Eat up, lass. You'll have to put some flesh on if you're going to work this croft with Thorfinn here. After we're gone, after we're gone.'

At that, another moan comes from the hunched woman in the fireside chair. It seems that twenty years have fallen on her in an hour. She looks once or twice with rage and bitterness at the girl from the sea, then she pokes up the peats and draws her chair closer up to the flames. Thorfinn can see her hands shivering.

The old man seems to get happier and younger as the hours pass. He has another mug of ale, then another.

'Hard work,' he says to Thorfinn, 'hard work for you, boy, teaching the lass to speak. Hard work, getting her used to the island and the island folk and their ways. Hard toil, instructing her in cheese-making and harvesting and spinning of wool. The good women round about, they'll show her the way, they'll teach her. For I reckon old Liza's too old for that.'

At that, his wife rises up from the chair and draws her shawl over her head and goes outside into the night.

'She'll come back, never fear,' says James Ragnarson. 'It's usually me that has to go to the ale-house of an evening to get some peace. She'll come back.'

Then the crofter says, 'I'm glad you've come to Ingle, lass.'

The girl looks at Thorfinn, then she looks at the old man, and she smiles, a new tremulous happy wondering light on her face.

James Ragnarson has a fourth mug of ale, and has lighted his pipe again.

'She must have come out of a shipwreck,' he says. 'There's no other way. It's a bit strange, though, the sea's been calm for a month and more now . . . We generally know, soon enough, when there's been a shipwreck. But there's been no word of a shipwreck, all the way from Fair Isle to Stroma . . . She'll tell us herself some day. The lass will tell us, once she has a mouthful of words . . . But I hope she never has such torrents of words as Liza or some of them other clattering women . . . Sleep? Where will she sleep? Mara will sleep in the barn, till we get a right bed for her. She won't be cold, there's plenty straw in the barn.'

At midnight, Thorfinn leads Mara to the barn, lighting the way with a lantern.

Then he goes down to the shore and fills two buckets with seawater and carries them up to the barn.

Going back to the croft house, he sees a shadow at the gable-end.

'Come in, mother,' he says. 'It's midnight. It's too cold for you out here.'

She turns from him. She seems to fold the shadows closer about her.

Inside, the old man is singing a stave of a ballad.

> I am a man upon the land,
> I am a selkie in the sea,
> And when I'm far from any strand,
> My home it is the Sule skerry.

That winter, Thorfinn and Mara were married in the kirk of Norday.

There were black whispers and wonderings among the islanders; especially the women's tongues were busy.

There had been no shipwreck, that much was sure. The woman must have been put ashore off a foreign ship – a castaway – and what kind of a woman would be set ashore on this island, without a silver piece in her purse, among strangers?

It was amazing, how quickly this bride of Thorfinn Ragnarson of Ingle picked up the language. Before the first snowdrops and daffodils she had enough words – Norse and Scots and English words mingled – to make herself understood. And she was so pleasant a young woman that even the bitterest gossips of Norday stilled their tongues. That idle young man of Ingle croft had gotten himself a good wife, wherever she had come from.

And moreover she mastered quickly all the tasks that a croft-wife has to do: milking the cow and butter-making

and cheese-making – fetching water from the well – card-
ing and spinning wool – digging peats at Beltane-time
from the dark hill – cooking broth and stews in the black
iron pots over the hearthflames – cleaning and filling the
oil lamps – baking oatcakes and barley bannocks on the
griddle – washing clothes in the burn.

And soon – it was obvious – there would be another
mouth to feed at Ingle. A young mother from the neighbouring farm of Smylder instructed Mara in the prep-
aration of the cradle and the swaddling clothes.

The old man of Ingle was delighted when he knew he
was going to be a grandfather soon. It had seemed to him
that such an idle dreamer as Thorfinn would be the end
of the Ragnarsons – after seven centuries the croft would
be taken over by strangers. But now, yes, the tree that
seemed to be all but dead was putting out new fresh
leaves.

The old man laughed over his mug in the ale-house that
night.

As for the mistress of Ingle, she dwined and grayed as
the winter came on. She had no relish in food or drink.
The torrent of words dried up in her – she, who had been
the most garrulous woman in Norday – until she only said
the necessary words, no more. And the clear ring was out
of her voice, it was like the rustle of wind through dry
grass. To her daugher-in-law she said never a word. She
went and lived in the ben-room, to avoid any contact with
Mara. They would meet from time to time, of course, at
the hearth or in the byre at milking-time, or at the gate
of the planticru. Then the old woman would mutter and
turn away quickly . . . At the end of winter, she took to
her bed, and lay looking at the stone wall, refusing food,
saying nothing. Thorfinn would listen at her door. Some-

times she was crying . . . But at the end of a fortnight she got out of bed. The girl that day had gone to visit Betsy Olafson in Smylder, who was teaching her to knit a fine white christening shawl, so delicate and light a garment it could (when finished) be drawn through a wedding ring.

The old woman came through to the room where James her man sat smoking his pipe. Thorfinn sat outside in the frost-bright air, knotting creels upon the wooden frames, a flat heavy sinking-stone on his knees. The boy was working well now, he had sloughed off all the errancy and laziness of his youth.

'Well,' said the wife of Ingle, 'now things are as they were. That witch has gone back where she came from. I'm mistress here at Ingle once more. And our boy will make a good farmer and fisherman. Oh, James, you'll get your beef and ale now the way you used to like them . . . I'm a lot better today, James. My tongue is loosened. I have a lot of winter work to do about this croft. I have so much to do I don't know where to begin . . .'

It seemed the torrent of words had exhausted her. She had to cling to the table. Her cheeks were like cinders with the last red glow in them . . . She struggled for breath. She pointed to the crib in the corner. 'What's that?' she whispered. 'Ah, well, now Thorfinn's learned to use his hands, I know just the right wife for him . . .' She mentioned the name of a spinster who lived alone at the edge of the moor. 'Yes, Jane Mosseter, she'll be mistress here after we're both gone, James. But that won't be for a long time yet.'

Someone went past the window. 'Tell the tinker wife I have no bread to give her today. Tell her to come back tomorrow,' she said.

Happy urgent voices mingled at the brigstones. The old woman went slowly to the door.

'My time has come,' said the girl from the sea. 'Oh hurry, is the bed ready? The bairn-clothes are in the kist. Willa the midwife is on her way. Betsy's gone to fetch her. I am very happy, man.'

Then Thorfinn kissed his wife, right there beside the window.

The old mother shuffled back slowly to her room.

That same afternoon a child was born, a son. There were cries of wonderment and joy in Ingle. Then, threading through all that delight, a thin wail. The heir was commenting, with sorrow, on the shore of time on which he had been stranded.

It was winter. In mid-afternoon, at sunset, Thorfinn carried his son in to let the grandmother see him.

There the old woman lay, with all her clothes on, on the bed.

And she lay so still, Thorfinn thought she must be dead.

The infant cried again. The old woman opened her eyes.

'Bless the bairn,' she whispered – and then again sought the silence. Her breath troubled a few white hairs at the corner of her mouth.

Thorfinn carried his precious freight back to the birth-room and handed the infant to the mother.

Five or six women were in Ingle now, come with gifts of cake and knitted things to the new child.

Willa the midwife was filling a cup with whisky.

The women were all speaking now in hushed voices.

Willa passed the cup of whisky to Thorfinn, then to the grandfather. They drank, solemnly. Willa poured water into the cup. Then she went over to the bed and dipped a finger in and put a drop of malt-and-water on the child's lip.

And he did not reject it.

'Thank the Best,' said Willa. 'He'll be a good farmer here at Ingle.'

Old James whispered to Thorfinn, 'How is it with her next door?'

And Thorfinn answered, 'She's content.'

But that same night, the old mistress of Ingle died. They buried her on the Wednesday. And on the Sunday following Magnus James Ragnarson was christened in the kirk of Norday. He gave a whimper or two at the sprinkling of water-drops, then he looked in wonderment at the faces round him, and smiled.

'Indeed,' says Willa the midwife, 'he'll catch a few thousand fish in his time, this one. He'll come through many a storm.'

For a few years, life went on happily enough at Ingle.

There were good harvests and poor harvests and middling harvests. Sometimes the sea was lavish with cod and lobsters, and sometimes stingy.

More children were born at Ingle, one every eighteen months or so, until at last there were five bairns, two boys and three girls.

One morning Mara came in from the well to find old James Ragnarson slumped in his chair. His pipe – the bowl still warm, a thread of tobacco smoke coming from it – lay broken on the flagstone. It had been an easy passage. They buried him beside his wife in the kirkyard, under a lichen-encrusted gravestone graven with the names of generations.

The daughter-in-law wept. Thorfinn comforted her. It

struck him that Mara's tears tasted saltier than the tears of other women and children. He said nothing of this to anyone.

But other islanders noticed, at harvest home or wedding or Johnsmas feast, that Mara would not eat the oatcakes and barley bannocks, nor so much as put her mouth to the ale-cog when it went round in a wide sun-wise circle . . . Thorfinn might have told them that, at home, neither would Mara eat the good earth-fruit, kale and turnips and potatoes. She could eat only food from the sea, herring and crab and haddock and skate, and whelks and mussels from the rockpools.

She sulked if her man came home from the sea with a poor catch. There was always of course a store of smoked fish and dried fish, but she liked her food better with the sea-silver fresh on it.

The dark mood never lasted long. The sight of her children flocking in at the door from flying a kite on the hilltop, or splashing among the dozen ducks in the burn, and the glad cry was in her mouth soon.

Ah, she loved her bairns as dearly as any mother in Norday. That cry of welcome! And yet it was unlike any other utterance, her speech and laughter and grief. The speech of the islanders has the earth-graining in it, a slow rise and fall, like furrows, like the drift of horses and cows across the hillside . . . Mara's speech had something of the music of breakers in a cave-mouth, or far-off horizon bell-notes, or dolphins in the flood tide.

And often she was down at the edge of the sea, looking westward. All island women do this, but only when there is a sudden storm and the fishing boats are out, and they stand there mute and cold about the lips; but more often it is a gossiping cheerful group of women at the boat noust

164

waiting with the gutting-knives and the straw caisies . . . But this Mara, she was down at the shore alone at all hours, shading her eyes westwards, when Thorfinn was out on the field with plough or harrows.

They noticed this well, the people of Norday. They noticed how she would run towards the skerry a mile away, across the wide curve of bay, when the seal-flock suddenly appeared there. The creatures looked at the woman stumbling over rocks and sand towards them. They eyed her coldly. Then one by one, they tumbled off the skerry into the sea, and drifted on the floodwaters, out and away from the island . . . She stood there, her hands up at her mouth.

But she was a good wife and a good mother. Except for a few women with tongues like thorns always, the island people all had a good word for her.

There was one very strange thing, though. The palms of the children's hands were covered with rough scales, not like the flower-soft hands of all the other island chil- dren. A fisherman mentioned this to Thorfinn down at the boat noust one morning: they were waiting for the wind to shift south a little, then they could sail out with their lines. 'No,' said Thorfinn, 'I don't have scaly hands – look . . .' The other fisherman shook his head. 'Maybe it comes from Mara's people . . .' 'It might and it might not,' said Thorfinn, 'but they won't burn their hands climbing with ropes on the crag. And they won't feel the crabs gripping them either . . .' He passed it off with a laugh. But he glared at the man he was going to fish with, and didn't speak to him all that day at sea. At night, though, they drank ale together in Kitty Fea's ale-house.

It was at full moon always, for three days or so, that the strangeness came on Mara.

165

One day Thorfinn came in hungry from the sheep-shearing. There was no dinner on the table. The children were drifting along the banks of the burn, plucking reeds to make little green boats with, to sail in the pool. Yes, they told their father, when he came from the empty house looking for them, their mother had sent them away and told them to come back at lamp-lighting time, she was too busy to attend to them, they would be all the hungrier for their supper. Thorfinn left them and went back to the house. There were signs of disturbance everywhere, clothes thrown from the cupboard, the blankets disturbed on the box-bed, the black iron pot and the stone salt jar and the jar of oil out of their places. But no sign in the house of Mara.

He found her in the barn, tearing at a bale of hay, her arms thrust in deep, and pale yellow wisps all about her feet.

'Is this the way to feed a hungry household?' he asked.

She looked at him. She brushed strands of hay from her hair and her apron. Without a word she went past him into the house, and poured water from a bucket into the black pot. The fire was almost out, a red core in the heart of gray peat embers. She knelt and blew it into flame. Then she brought down the jar of oatmeal to make the porridge for supper, whenever the water began to bubble and sing.

Thorfinn lit the lamp. Then he went to the door and called the children home.

The dew was falling. Thorfinn wiped his hands in the long grass, to rid them of the oil of shearing.

When the children came running in, breathless, six bowls and six horn spoons were on the table, waiting for the hot salted porridge to be ladled in.

Mara took a pair of dried sillocks from the wall outside and set them on her own plate. She would not eat porridge.

The family had grown accustomed to their mother's silences at the moon's rounding out, and for three or four days they would move about the house, silent and uneasy themselves.

Their father said, as the heavy rich incense of porridge drifted across the table, 'The Lord make us truly thankful.'

Then, one morning, Mara was singing again. The house was full of happiness. The youngest two clung to her skirts with their rough scarred hands. Their mother had been restored to them.

They came home with armfuls of iris and meadowseet, and she put them in clay pots here and there, in the little dark cottage.

And Thorfinn went out to round up a few stray sheep that had ragged coats.

There was one frightful day at Ingle, the like of which had never been . . . (God forbid it should ever be again!)

It was an idle day in Norday, too soon for ploughing (for the scars of snow were still on the flank of Fea the hill, and there were only a few hours of light on either side of noon) and there had been poor fishing for days.

Thorfinn went down early to the fishing-bothy, and was there with a dozen young men. They usually played at draughts, or argued, or told stories. Then, in the twilight of late afternoon they would go home, smouldering with impatience, some of them at a day wasted, others uncaring one way or the other – for spring always comes, quite suddenly some years, and then it is once more time to wipe the spiders'-webs from the ploughs and to patch the creels . . . That afternoon, in the darkening, a group of young Norday men came up from the shore, laughing and shouting, carrying a burden – it looked like a freighted sack from the distance, or a long heavy stone. Where were they taking the thing, whatever it was? One man pointed to Ingle, the nearest farm. Thorfinn would have none of that. The little company drew nearer. The farmer of Smylder went down to meet them with a lantern. The stars were coming out, in the frosty air they seemed to be snapping their fingers. So, the young men, Thorfinn among them, turned with their burden to Smylder. And they set it down on the brigstones outside, and the women coming to see what all the song and dance was about saw that the arms of the fishermen were splashed red, and the blood clots had soiled their jerseys . . . Then Mara Ragnarson crossed the field to bring her man home; the porridge was growing cold in the pot. She pushed through the group of women. She looked, she stood in silence for a moment, then she screamed and hurled herself at Thorfinn, she tore at his beard, she made furrows down his cheek with her nails, she made her hands fists and beat him about the face and body. He gripped her hands, he held her away from him so that she couldn't kick him any more. But still she screamed, not in words anyone there could recognize, but like a trapped animal. It was terrible! The women, and some of the men, were white in the face. A few made little gestures with their hands, as much as to say, 'Now now, let there be peace . . . No need for a hullabaloo like this . . .' Mara flailed at the air with her free foot, and screamed again . . . One or two islanders turned and hurried home.

Thorfinn covered her mouth with his hand, and winced at the fierce bite she gave him, but still gagged her with his fingers; then he lifted her, thrashing, into his arms and went blundering with her across the field to Ingle . . . At the door of Ingle the five children were weeping. Thorfinn told them to go to the Glebe – Janet Kerrigan would warm them at her fire. Their mother was not well, she would soon be better, he would come and fetch them from Glebe farm with a lantern, later. 'Go, now . . .'

The children went – anywhere to be away from all that rage and terror.

And Thorfinn Ragnarson carried his wife indoors and threw her, moaning gently now, on the bed.

The children did not go to the Glebe. They daren't tear themselves away from their distracted mother and their stricken father. They lingered about the door of Ingle. The sobbing inside went on, but brokenly, and they heard their father's low voice, gentle sorrowful reassuring words.

At last there was silence.

The lamp was lit in the window.

The coldness of the thousand stars was in the blood of the children. The oldest lifted the latch and went in, quietly, followed by his brothers and sisters.

The fire was purring and snoring and putting out bright claws on the hearth. Their father was stirring the porridge pot above the flames.

He had washed the blood from his hands. He had put off the clotted blue jersey and put on a gray one. They looked curiously at his torn face.

He pointed with his wooden spoon at the figure on the bed.

Their mother was sleeping.

The room was full of an under-sea peace.

Back at Smylder they were still aghast and half speech-less. All that insane rage, because a sea-beast, a seal, had been killed! A fine fat creature too – they would get three or four pairs of shoes from the hide, a dozen jars of oil maybe. They wouldn't eat it, the flesh was too tough. But Tammo of Westvoe, he said he wouldn't mind making a pot of stew from the trotters.

They came back again and again to the distracted rage of Mara of Ingle! Surely it was madness, Thorfinn Ragnarson marrying a foreign castaway woman like her, not knowing anything at all about her forebears or her circumstances.

'And yet,' said Sam Olafson of Smylder, 'she's a fine lass, Mara.'

Another winter and spring and summer passed.

In the croft of Ingle all was harmony once more. In fact, there had never been such peace and contentment there.

It had been a good year at the fishing and on the land. Once the rent had been paid at the factor's office, there were a few sovereigns and crown pieces to lay in the kist under the bed.

There was even a bonus. A westerly gale in early summer drove a Swedish ship on the rocks. The crew struggled through the waves to the shore, and were lodged in crofts here and there till they were taken away by a ship sent from Leith. The crofters were well compensated for giving lodging and comfort – they were told it was 'insurance money', whatever that meant. They and the wrecked sailors discovered they had even some words in common. How could that be, when a great ocean separates Orkney from Sweden?

Only the skipper wandered disconsolate every day round the shore, searching here and there. His young wife had been on the ship, and though Bjorn Thorsteen had

glimpsed her once or twice in the boiling seas of shipwreck, and had tried to get to her, in the end a combing
wave and smother of foam had gone over her head, and
he did not see her again.

He searched up and down the coast, from dawn to sunset, but there was no sign of her. He pleaded with the
farmer of Toft where he was being put up to get him a
lantern, so that he could search in the darkness. They
persuaded him that it would be a waste of time. Besides,
he was exhausted, physically and mentally.

When the ship from Leith came to take the Swedes on
the first stage of their journey home, Bjorn Thorsteen
pleaded to be allowed to stay a few days more in the
island. Tomorrow he would find his young wife for sure.
She might even be alive, living in a cave somewhere on
raw limpets and the little rills of fresh water that often
drip from cave roofs.

It showed how far gone in grief the poor man was, that
such an impossible hope fluttered in his heart. In the end
his crewmen had almost to carry Bjorn Thorsteen on to
the Leith ship.

The laird, as soon as word came to the Hall that the
Malmo had been wrecked on the Gray Head, sent word
by the factor to every house in Norday that the cargo
belonged to the crown; therefore any attempt at plun-
dering the wreck would be very severely punished. But
by the time Elphinstone rode round with this edict, nearly
the entire cargo – Swedish timber and casks of Finnish
vodka – had been stowed away in places secret from those
in authority for generations and centuries, under old derelict foundations, in the caves half-way up the crags –
inaccessible to all but a few initiates – where the young
men had hidden from the press-gang.

Elphinstone knew well enough why there were more drunk men than usual in Norday that summer; also why so many new fishing-boat keels were being laid and clean strakes fitted, and new doors set in croft-house and barn, but there was nothing he could do about it. He let it be known, though, that in view of the increased value of the holdings, the rents would be going up as from Martinmas first.

It was Thorfinn Ragnarson, looking for mussel-bait in the ebb, who turned a swathe of seaweed and found the body. There was little left of it. From the abundance of golden hair, there was little doubt that it was Solveig Thorsteen, the Swedish skipper's wife.

She was buried next day in the kirkyard.

The laird wrote a letter to the Swedish consul in Edinburgh.

It was August, the time of the Lammas Fair.

Seeing that it had been a fairly successful summer Thorfinn suggested to Mara that they all go to the Fair, leaving in Abraham Rosey's longboat *Falcon* at first light and coming back at nightfall. The children were excited. At the Fair they would be given 'fairings', there would be apples and cinnamon water and liquorice, and half of Orkney would be there, in the fairground under the huge red cathedral of St Magnus. There would be fiddles and dancing and a clown and a man with a monkey and a black African prince. The children at Ingle had never been to a Lammas Fair before. They were beside themselves. Even in their beds, Mara could hardly hush them to sleep. It would be a day of utter enchantment.

Mara said that of course she wouldn't be going. Some-one had to stay and milk Meadowsweet and Moondrift the two cows. And the hens must be fed, and the fire must never be allowed to go out (when the fire goes out, a house begins to die).

Oh, she had plenty to do at Ingle, Mara assured Thorfinn. She smiled. It would be good to have one day of perfect peace, all by herself with the animals. She pressed her man's hand. Thorfinn had not known her so tranquil.

The children were so excited they would hardly touch their breakfast. Their faces glowed with cold water and rough towelling. They scarcely had patience to bid their mother farewell. They turned and ran helter-skelter down to the beach where a score of other islanders were gathered, and Abraham Rosey was waiting with the rope in his hand beside the *Falcon*.

And the mother: for the first time ever she had broken an oatcake and dipped it in the honey-jar, and half lifted it to her mouth – a thing she had never done before. But at the very last moment her appetite refused the morsel. She put it back on the table. Two solitary tears glittered in her eyes.

Thorfinn kissed his wife, a thing he generally did only at New Year. He tasted tears twice as salt as the grief or joy of the other Norday women.

He said then, 'I think maybe we shouldn't go at all. There's still a dozen sheep to be shorn. A pity to waste such a good day.'

It was too late. The children were calling him from the shore, urgently. 'Come on, father! Hurry! Abraham can't wait any more. What's wrong with you?'

'Go, man, now,' said Mara.

And the sea-creatures and the land-creatures and the birds of the air urged him: 'Go.'

Oh, it was a hearty boatload of Norday people who

came home that evening! The women's baskets were over-flowing with the goods they'd bought in the Kirkwall shops – Spanish oranges, cherry cakes, boiled toffee, printed ballads and broadsheets: things never seen in Norday before. The young men and women were clustered in the stern, whispering secretly and urgently as if they were in some wonderful conspiracy known only to the young, and one youth, Sander Kerrigan of the Glebe gave Jenny Sinclair a little box of sweetmeats, and she lifted her mouth to his mouth, between a laugh and a blush. And 'tut-tut' clucked the farm-wives, at such shamelessness. Thorfinn Ragnarson had not a care in the world – he was mildly merry with whisky, he had a silver brooch wrought in a barley-stalk shape for Mara – handsome she'd look going to the kirk on Sabbath with that brooch holding her shawl at the throat – and the five children were a bit fretful and sleepy after the excitements of the day . . .

The passengers came ashore, the men with their breeches rolled above the knee carrying the long-skirted women from sea to rock and sand. Plenty of shriekings and laughter and reprovings from the womenfolk young and old. Thorfinn made two sallies ashore, with a child on each shoulder, and the second time with the youngest – Sam – in his arms asleep . . . There would be a good supper on the table for them, porridge and warm milk, but the three youngest would want nothing but their bed, after goodnight kisses from their mother.

There was no light in the window, and that was a bit strange, for now in late August the shadows were gathering thicker and sooner. And the lamps were shining from all the other windows in Norday.

Also the cow Meadowsweet was lowing distractedly in the field, as if it was long past milking-time.

174

The door was open.

Thorfinn bade the children wait at the planticru wall – one of them had begun to wail – he went inside. Mara was not there, and the fire that had burned in the hearth ever since the croft-house was built was almost out – there was only one live ember, a dull redness at the heart of the ashes. Thorfinn took a peat from the basket, broke it, and set the fragments about the dying ember. (If a hearth-fire goes out, the whole household is under threat . . .) Besides, there must always be someone at home – a croft should never be left empty – there must always be breath in the house . . . And 'Mara' he called twice more, not too loud for fear of upsetting the children.

There was no answer. The croft-wife was no longer there, neither in the ben-room nor the but-room, not in byre or barn or stable, there was no shadow on the hill road, and below there was only the sound of the darkling sea . . . And then, among the rinsings and echoings of the sea on the shore, he thought he heard a new cry.

He left the wailing and lamentation of the children, who seemed to know that now they were motherless forever, and ran down to the shore, the very stretch of sand where a dozen years before, he had seen the seal dance.

The beach was empty. A company of dark shadows upon the darkening ebb – the seals were drifting out to the open ocean. One of the seals called to him, but the very sound of his name was strange in that ocean language. It was a strange terrible cry, of love and loss, joy and longing.

Thorfinn stayed at the shore till midnight. Then he went home. His eldest son, Magnus, had lit the lamp. The fire had not gone out, after all, the flames were putting red tongues about a new-laid peat. Two of the children had gone to bed. Two had fallen asleep in the straw chairs.

'Is our mother drowned?' said Magnus.

'No,' said the father, 'she isn't drowned. She's gone to visit some of her people. She may be home in the morning. We must be patient.'

When all the children were in bed, Thorfinn lit the lantern and climbed the ladder into the loft. He knew exactly where he had left the sealskin: in his great-grandfather's sea-chest with the heavy brass padlock on it. And the iron key was on the cobwebbed rafter above, in the angle where the lowest roof-stone begins to tilt.

The contents of the chest were scattered about the loft; there was no sign of the sealskin.

Thorfinn Ragnarson fell asleep in the loft, between a mariner's chart and a few Pictish stone axeheads found long ago in a peat-bank.

He was wakened soon after dawn by a shout from below, 'Thorfinn, are you there, man? Hurry! There's no time to waste . . .'

The children were still asleep.

Thorfinn opened the door to Andrew Olafson of Smylder. 'Thorfinn, they're back. The press-gang. They're up at the laird's house. They came in the darkness. They'll start combing the island within the hour. We're going to the caves now, at once. Hurry . . .'

Thorfinn Ragnarson shook his head. No, he wouldn't come. Let the press-gang take him if they wanted him. But he wished safety and peace to the other young men of Norday.

Andrew Olafson gaped at him as if he were an idiot.

'Not come with us?' he said. 'How will Mara manage

the croft without you, man? There are the five bairns to provide for. Come on, hurry. I hear the horses prancing about in the laird's yard already.'

'Be off with you, Andrew,' said Thorfinn. 'There are bairns to feed and two cows to be milked. The press-gang might come, they might not come. It will be a change for me, maybe, to fight against the king's enemies.'

*　　*　　*

Thorfinn – the twentieth-century Thorfinn – was wakened from his two-hundred-year-old dream by the wet muzzle of Selkie the horse. The sun was down. The island hollows brimmed with shadow.

Selkie was tired of the rough grass here at the top of Fea hill. This rider was too much of a lazybones and a dreamer for Selkie. Selkie wanted to drink the winds in their courses, his hooves whirling and throbbing across the island.

Together they rode down the hill track to the road that circled the island.

There was a light in the window of Ingle.

Thorfinn dismounted and let the horse loose in the field.

He glanced through the window. There at the table sat his father and Tina Lyde; Tina was taking a cake and pots of jam out of her basket; the kettle was beginning to steam and sputter on the stove, and the teapot was warming on the hob. The table was set for three.

Tina Lyde seemed confused when Thorfinn came in. But Thorfinn gave her a civil greeting, and then Tina was all cheerfulness and goodwill. The father looked happy and anxious by turns.

'Ragna's gone away for a few days,' he said. 'Old Ben Hoy's fallen and broken his leg. Ragna's looking after him till he can walk again. Dr Lamond asked her would she go. We'll manage by ourselves.'

'Ragna's a right good-hearted lass,' said Tina Lyde, with a bit too much enthusiasm. 'You won't either of you want for food or fire. Everything'll work out fine.'

'It'll have to,' said Thorfinn mildly. 'The things we plan for always turn out different, and not always for the worse, though we might have a heavy heart now and again.'

'This is ham I cured myself,' said Tina, putting thick slices on Matthew's plate and Thorfinn's plate. 'The bannocks I made this afternoon.'

'Thank you,' said Thorfinn.

Aerodrome

NEXT MORNING A huge cargo-ship anchored off Norday.

Labourers from Scotland and Ireland were ferried ashore and began at once to erect a little village of Nissen huts in the open meadow between the village and the hill. The ship's crane swung barrels and steel sheets, bags of cement and sand, pre-fabricated doors, baulks of timber, crates of beer and boxes of bread and tinned meat and fish and soup, out of the hold into four deep-draughted boats.

The workmen, whenever they paused from the work of unloading and carrying and building, looked at Norday and its soil and sea and sky as if they had been sentenced to Devil's Island or Spitzbergen or Rockall.

But once the beer canteen was erected beside the Glebe hayfield, they began to look happier. The music of Donegal and of Clydeside was heard in Norday for the first time.

The whole island had come down to gape at this invasion.

Another larger ship was sighted off the headland, steaming towards the bay.

'We're going to get a pier out of this,' said Thomas Vass. 'A fine new big pier. It'll have to be. I told them so.'

Simon Taing demanded of the factor what he was going to do. He was waving a letter he had just got at the shop and post office kept by Isa Estquoy. He had received word to vacate Bu farm within the month, himself and his family and livestock. His land was being requisitioned by the government. And not only his land – just at harvest time too – but the farm of the Glebe, that was being taken over, and Ingle croft and Smylder too, two-thirds of the good island of Norday was being reft from them: the most fertile land. Letters had come for six farmers.

'The government!' said Thomas Vass. 'National security. Too intricate for the likes of you to take in. But don't worry – never fear – you'll be compensated, all of you, beyond your wildest dreams. You'll be the wealthiest men in Orkney.'

John Kerrigan of the Glebe made to strike the factor, he was so enraged.

'Nothing to do with me,' said Thomas Vass. 'I didn't open the island to them. Nor did Mr Harcourt-Smithers either. They may be taking over the Hall too, to be some sort of headquarters. So I've been informed.'

More workmen were ferried ashore. Foremen shouted orders. Dogs barked at farm ends, and hammers rang. Tents like mushrooms appeared at the edge of the site: for a few nights the operators would have to camp until the complex of huts was ready to receive them.

The beer canteen was almost finished and stocked by noon: the first fruit in this steel harvest.

'What about me?' cried James MacTavish from the inn door. 'They'll ruin me with their wet canteen. I never heard of this lot getting a licence from the licensing court in Kirkwall. This inn is the only licensed premises in the island . . .' Louis Stewart let his bull go free in the barleyfield of Westvoe. Louis Stewart was a gloomy fate-touched man – he foresaw that bread and ale were never to be tasted next winter. It was worse than hurricane or earthquake. But that was the way of it. There was nothing to be done.

Thomas Vass took a few of the older islanders aside. 'I'm not sure,' he said, 'I can't swear to it, but there are reliable reports that the requisitioned farms are to become a fighter aerodrome. Imagine that, if you can. A month from now, and Norday will be changed beyond anything we can imagine. We will be a fortress in the ocean, a very important place. It has to be, it has to be. No use complaining. Only remember this, we'll be wealthy men because of it. This island has known poor times in the past. All that is over. There are other islands. You can buy good farms there. Or we can retire and take our ease in Kirkwall or Hamnavoe.'

Matthew Ragnarson stood all that day in the door of his barn, watching the furious activity below. There was a letter in his hand too. His land had been surveyed the year before, of course. Even as he looked, five workmen came and tore down his meadow fences. Tina Lyde was suddenly there, at his side. 'Go away, woman,' he said. 'Leave me alone.'

The Ingle dog, Stalwart, curled behind the men demolishing the fence and went for one of them and bit him in the leg. There was a burst of Irish rage and a heavy boot thudded into the dog's side and it yowled. Matthew called it back. He returned, whimpering. 'Put a chain on your wolf,' shouted Declan O'Flaherty.

Meantime the second larger ship the *More* had anchored closer to the beach and great sections of wood were levered out of her open stern and fitted into place, with baulks and iron bolts, and soon a ramp led straight from the ship to the shore. Down this inclined plane came tractors, bulldozers, vans, and trucks. Arc-lamps were set up, and near sundown powerful lights were focused on the path leading up from the sand to the road. Already a score of men had set to work widening the fishermens' path with blocks of concrete. There were huge drums of tar and crates of metalling chips. A bad-tempered man, holding a kind of chart, instructed the gang of navvies. Whenever this civil engineer shouted too loud, the Glasgow men would down tools and go up to the beer canteen that was already selling bottles of Guinness and MacEwan's and the Donegal men would sit on the rocks and light their pipes and wait till the boy with the rag round his neck returned with a full case of stout. And then the director of operations, red in the face, would return to a small office that had been bolted together already and discuss the situation with two other officials there. At last one of the contractors – not the bad-tempered hectoring one – would come up and exchange a few words under an arc-lamp with a trade unionist from Wishaw, and soon afterwards the labourers knocked the embers from their pipes and wiped the froth from their mouths, and work on the shore road resumed.

The island rang with noise and shouting and clangour all night long. Few of the farmers and fishermen slept the night out. 'Oh indeed,' wailed Bella Simpson, 'it was all prophesied long ago in Revelations, and in the book of

Daniel too.' More arc-lights were turned on between the hills. The stars were cinders.

The only happy man in Norday was Jimmo Greenay the beachcomber. He wandered between groups of navvies and labourers and was given a cigarette here and the dregs of a beer bottle there. The cook-house was in full operation soon after midnight. There Jimmo was given a hot dog and a bottle of Coke – he didn't like them, but he ate and drank (as always) whatever was put before him. 'This is a lot better than the Hamnavoe Lammas Fair,' said Jimmo. One of the security men saw him at the door of the canteen, and shouted, 'What's that man doing here?' . . . Then Jimmo was taken to the little office on the sea banks and interrogated by three men. He was never so frightened in all his life; he didn't understand what the strangers were saying, they might as well have been speaking Chinese . . . At last they decided he wasn't a spy, and let him go, with a warning not to go near the site again – only islanders with official cards could get past the gate.

The islanders saw, in the early hours, the lights of a third ship, then a fourth, anchored out in the Sound.

The new village of Nissen huts was half completed when the islanders came to their doors next morning before breakfast.

Bulldozers and lorries loaded with empty water-tanks were coming down the ramp.

The men with the charts were measuring beside the burn now – it was divulged to Thomas Vass that a small reservoir was to be constructed; a twice-daily water-ship would be inconvenient.

Six of the island fishing-boats had been commandeered to bring a few score more craftsmen and labourers from ship to shore, and the fishermen were handed, at the little office, generous promissory notes. The *Scallop*, drawn high up the noust, was regarded as being too derelict for service.

The bulldozers were in action already, scooping up a sheepfold and a hill bothy, here and there: a preliminary demolition. Those minor buildings that had always been there, like the stars and the skerries, were uprooted in an hour. The islanders felt as if a piece of themselves had died.

The phone in the little office rang every two minutes or so, like some insane creature. 'It's a telephone, of course,' said Thomas Vass at the inn bar that morning. 'The laird was speaking of getting one in at the Hall next summer . . .' Even the post office didn't have a telephone.

'Worse than the Shanghai waterfront,' said Ben Hoy to Ragna Ragnarson as she was bringing him his tea and toast. 'I'd give them something to think about, the scum, if I hadn't broken my leg . . .' Ben Hoy was eating the last of his toast when Geordie Wylie came in with a letter. (Geordie Wylie was the Norday postman as well as the gravedigger.) The letter advised Benjamin Hoy, Esquire, of Lookout Cottage, Norday, Orkney, that his house and lands appertaining and contingent were required for purposes of national security, and Mr Hoy would oblige by removing himself and his belongings before the end of the month. Adequate compensation, and more, would be paid in due course, in consideration of the inconvenience caused to the householder.

Ben Hoy was a bad patient: he grumbled and complained all the time on account of the pain in his broken leg. But the cry he vented after Ragna had read the letter came from otherwhere. Ben Hoy, when he retired from

184

sea, had restored Lookout with his own hands. But his forebears had lived on the same site for generations.

'I wonder if they'll uproot the kirkyard,' said Geordie Wylie the postman-gravedigger, leaving Lookout. He had a half-dozen similar letters to deliver to houses here and there that morning.

Doctor Hector Lamond did not have a telephone either: what good would a telephone have done when none of the other islanders had a telephone? The hospital in Kirkwall had urged him for two years and more to install a telephone, but he hadn't got down to it yet. He liked better to be awakened by a clatter of midnight hooves, and a fistful of gravel against the window. Dr Lamond was having his ham and eggs and breakfast coffee when a barbaric thundering came at his door – a new sound to him, since most of the islanders, in daylight hours, gave a gentle tap; even though it might be a summons to a stroke or a bull-goring. 'Sure,' said the site foreman when the doctor opened the door, 'they're after murtherin' each other, Jock and Pat. You might be in time to save them and you might not . . .' It had been a drunken brawl in the new corrugated-iron canteen. Two of the site-workers had gone for each other, one with a broken bottle, the other with great fists like lumps of Connemara marble . . . When Dr Lamond got there, the combatants were shaking hands and pouring beer in each other's glasses. A dozen stitches closed up the bloody flap on the side of Conor Murphy's head; the doctor thought Gerry Watson's nose was broken beyond reconstituting. The fighters insisted on giving Dr Lamond a pound note each, a larger fee than he had ever received in Norday before . . .

An hour later Conor Murphy and Gerry Watson were working side by side, putting up still more Nissen huts for the still inflowing builders of the aerodrome to stay in.

Now all of Norday knew what was going to happen: all that fertile part of the island between the hill and the shore was to be laid out in runways and hangars, so that the German bombers, if they ever flew over Scapa Flow to attack the battle fleet anchored there would, themselves cumbersome and slow, be engaged by swift leaf-light lancing fighter planes, the toreadors of the sky.

At noon a bulldozer went at the old disused mill built beside the burn. Matthew Ragnarson's uncle had once been the miller there. Now in two hours the mill was uprooted, the stones were scattered in a cloud of red-brown dust. The huge millstones were dragged away by tractors to be broken up . . . The ducks from the millpond went squawking across the fields.

It wasn't possible for Mr Simon to do much teaching in the school that day, the island was full of such clamour and clangour. Besides, the children were too excited to think of multiplication tables and the kings and queens of Scotland. When finally Mr Simon let them go half an hour early, they found in the village another delight. Isa Estquoy, whose shop also had had an order to quit imposed on it, was offering her stock free of charge to anyone who called. Jimmo Greenay's pockets bulged with tins of corned beef and sardines. The school kids thronged like berserkers among the sweetie jars. James MacTavish, the richest man in the island, was shameless enough to come away from Isa Estquoy's shop with a sackful of lemonade and raspberry crush in bottles. In case anyone fancied lacing their whisky with that coloured gasiness!

But strangely enough the same counter and desk where she sold stamps and weighed parcels of wool and salt cod and cashed old-age pensions, the post office part of the

establishment, was regarded as necessary and was to con-
tinue until further notice – but the grocery and post office
were so knit together that it was impossible to see just
how they could be disentangled. Isa Estquoy decided that
the shop would have to be discontinued – stamps and
postal orders, being government business, were obviously
much more important.

In late afternoon a wing-commander and other officers
were met at the shore by Thomas Vass and driven to the
Hall. The officers examined the big house carefully, room
by room – consulted with each other for a quarter-hour
in the overblown garden – and then let the factor know
that the place, with some reconstitution, would be suitable
as living-quarters for pilots and crews. Would Mr Vass
see to it that any furniture or ornaments or works of art,
of any value, were inventoried and removed and stored
in a safe place? Then Mr Vass drove them back to the
launch that had brought them.

What was this, in the early evening, a haystack fire at
Westvoe farm? From the village a mile away a rag of
flame shook in the wind. Then there were red rags and
yellow rags of fire from the thatch and barn and roof-tree
of Westvoe. The Westvoe cattle went in a stampede
through the new village of Nissen huts. Some of the
labourers barred themselves in the wet canteen as the
hooves went thundering through – a few crazy labourers
tried to mount the beasts and ended up in pools of cement
or in the churned-up mud. Finally Matthew Ragnarson
and Howie Ayre the quarryman and Jock Seatter the blacksmith and their dogs, rounded the fire-crazed herd up
before they went over the sea banks. The farmer of
Westvoe took no part in saving his beasts.

The eight-hundred-year old farm was destroyed by the

fire. And what had caused it? 'I knocked over the lamp,' said Louis Stewart of Westvoe, 'and the curtain caught . . .' But how could one upset lamp have caused fire to break out in five places at once: haystack and barn and dwellinghouse?

'I hope you're well insured,' said Thomas Vass. But no, Louis Stewart hadn't thought about insurance – he nor his father nor his grandfather before him. In fact, he seemed to think that there was something wrong about defending a farm against tempest or fire with *money*.

The Stewart family were given sanctuary in the empty Manse.

That night everybody in MacTavish's stood Louis Stewart of Westvoe whisky. When he got drunk near midnight he said, 'Better a clean fire than to be choked with paper and fumes and rust . . .'

Amid all this whirl of clangour, uprooting, confusion, pulverization, fire, Winnie Swona and her granddaughter Eliza went on with their work, up there on the flank of the hill in the poor croft of Swinhurst. Swinhurst was out of range of the proposed flightpath; no official order had been attached to Winnie Swona's place. Grannie and granddaughter fed their hens and milked the goat and scythed their grass and weeded their tatties, on two green patches on the dark moor.

Three of their hens disappeared one night – the next night Winnie Swona stood guard over the henhouse with a pitchfork. A shadow moved in the darkness. Winnie struck, and struck. There was a curse and a yell, the plash of boots stumbling over the marsh back to the camp. A half-strangled cockerel lay fluttering in the yard.

The seals, a placid company all that summer on the skerry, suddenly one morning took the tide and sought sanctuary in another island. The five larks, also, seemed to have left the Norday sky. They were not seen again in Norday that year.

The wireless in MacTavish's inn announced one evening that the Prime Minister, Neville Chamberlain, had flown back to London from a meeting with Adolf Hitler in Munich. Mr Chamberlain waved a piece of paper to the anxious crowd at the airport, bearing the signature of himself and the German Chancellor. 'Peace in our time,' he said in his undertaker's voice. 'Out of the nettle of danger I have plucked the flower of safety . . .'

The Londoners were wild with joy.

'Good,' said MacTavish, rubbing his hands. 'There'll soon be an end to this nonsense here in Norday. They'll pack and go quicker than they came. What has Scotland to do, anyway, with their European quarrels? The sooner that drunken rabble is out of the island . . .' MacTavish gave the four men in the bar a glass of whisky each, for nothing, that night: a thing never known before.

Howie Ayre the quarryman said, 'Norway ought to declare war on Scotland for stealing Orkney from them five hundred years ago.'

'Don't talk nonsense, man,' said James MacTavish. 'Drink up your whisky now and be thankful.'

Mr Chamberlain's dove-flight from Munich seemed to make no difference to the construction work at the aerodrome. If anything, it went forward more urgently than before. Two more cargo ships anchored off the island, a hundred more navvies arrived on the *Raven*. The *Raven* was doing well, ferrying workers and officials twice every day.

Rocks were dynamited off-shore the day after the Prime Minister spoke; the whole island shuddered to the roots with the noise; it seemed they were going to build a pier as Thomas Vass had predicted at Norday; engineers in clean overalls went here and there with charts and measuring rods; one, standing knee-deep in the sea, slipped in the seaweed and broke his ankle; he would have drowned in a rockpool if Jimmo Greenay hadn't dragged him out by the scruff of the neck. Dr Lamond was brusque with this gaffer; he gave a yell or two, being bandaged – a thing not known before in any of Dr Lamond's ministrations.

The grannie and granddaughter up at Swinhurst didn't even turn their heads as the explosions went on and on for a week. There they stood against the dawnlight, hoes in hand. It seemed those two might have arrived soon after the first thunderous fracturing of the ice-cap, ten thousand years before, keepers of the first green shoots.

A man in a bowler-hat with a brief-case called at the inn one day. 'Leave me alone,' shouted MacTavish. 'I want nothing to do with you! You're ruining me, that's what. The island men are going to your wet canteen now; it's a den of iniquity that place. No gambling or housie-housie in Norday before you lot came.'

The man from the Ministry said coldly, 'How many rooms do you have in this inn? Could I see your register? It amounts to this, we might have to take over your inn within the next month, certain key workers have to be accommodated. You'll be doing your country a service. You won't be the poorer for it. Thank you for your co-operation. Good day.'

MacTavish said not a word for the rest of that day. In the early evening he closed the bar and went up to his room. The next morning Billie Holm, the porter and odd-job man, found him dead in his bed.

A ship arrived that afternoon. Six bulldozers and ten lorries rolled down the ramp.

The *Raven* arrived with three young lady typists and a flight-sergeant and two pilot-officers. The workmen, busy on a dining-hall-cum-cinema, whistled and cheered. A small Nissen hut accommodated the typists. Mabel from the inn cooked and cleaned for them and made their beds. The chattering of typewriters was added to the new sounds of Norday.

An old grass-clad quarry that had been abandoned two generations before was resurrected, to provide road metalling. The island shook with more explosions. Birds flew up out of the quarry ledges and pools and wheeled in the dusty wind and flew away to far cliffs and lochans.

One night – the same night that three bulldozers crushed the uncut barley of the Glebe into a green slush, after a day of rain – there was a red sunset, and the horse Selkie was seen on the summit of the hill against the crimson splendour. Then another raincloud covered the sun, a shower drove in out of the west over the hill and the island. When Matthew Ragnarson looked again from the door of Ingle, after the cloud passed, the horse was no longer there.

When Matthew went to rouse Thorfinn next morning for his bowl of porridge, the young man's room was empty, and the old sea-chest was gone from under the bed.

It seemed that Thorfinn Ragnarson had left the island, perhaps for ever.

191

Fisherman
and Croftwoman

THE OLD BOAT is almost seaworthy again. The man has worked on her for a week and more, patching and caulking and painting. The name of the boat has faded on the stern. Now the man sits, freshening the name with white paint – SCALLOP.

The small hut above the beach has been attended to already. A new pane glitters in the seaward-facing window. A board has been renewed here and there to keep out rats and birds. There are stipplings of tar here and there. It's plain, this restoration has not happened a day too soon . . . Another winter, and both boat and hut would be beyond repair.

A sea-haar has crept in overnight and covered the island. The island of Selskay across the Sound appears ghost-like sometimes, then a minute later is completely blotted out.

The sea is ebbing. It lapped the shore pebbles two hours before when the man was having his breakfast of porridge and tinned milk. Now it is edging out, leaving fringes of seaweed and rock studded with limpets, and the melancholy sounds a shrinking sea makes. A lost sea bird shrieks out in the Sound.

It won't be time for fishing for a week at least. There are still the score of lobster creels to be patched. It will not be easy. The man has worked creels, in a way, a long while ago, but then only as a boy who had come to bail and tie lobster claws; and then little was expected of, or hoped for, from a dreamer like him. 'Ah well,' says the man to the mournful fog-lost bird, 'let's hope the blood of a few generations remembers . . .'

The man speaks to himself often, or to an off-shore seal, or to the nesting fulmars, or to a rabbit who has come to nibble at the turf on the links above.

There is no one else in Norday to talk to. The island is utterly deserted.

There: the name has been painted on the boat. 'That's enough for one morning,' he says to the gull that has just furled on the chimney-head of his hut. 'Time to speak to the ghosts.'

It is a cold clinging fog. He puts on his duffle coat in the hut, then adds some driftwood to the glow in the rusty stove. 'Thank you for the use of your house, Jimmo,' he says, closing the door. 'In winter, I'll have to look for a place with thicker walls. But where? There's nothing where Ingle was, not a stone.'

On the road above the beach, the full desolation can be seen. There is a mile-long runway where were once the farms of Glebe, Bu, Westvoe, Smylder, Ingle. Grass and weeds are growing through every fissure. There are skeletons of two big hangars, doorless and roofless. Concrete has set its lasting blight on a thousand years of fertility. 'This land will never be unlocked,' says the man to a

194

crow walking in blackness on the edge of the runway. The crow flies off. 'The concrete will still be there at the next return of the ice.'

It is melancholy, the deserted village. The roofs sag, most of the windows are cracked, the doors that haven't been torn off withered. It can just be read, the sign over the inn door – 'Norday Inn, licd. to sell wines, ales, spirits. Prop: Jas. MacTavish' . . . A crate of empty beer bottles stands at the door still.

The solitary islander looks through the webbed and stained bar window. The interior seems sunk in an underseas mirk. An axe has been taken to the heavy bar counter and one end has been hacked away raggedly. The mirror over the gantry is still there, with the portrait of Burns on it and the quotation in florid Victorian lettering, 'Freedom and whisky gang together, tak aff yer dram': but all dark and tarnished.

On a shelf of the post office once kept by Isa Estquoy is the small metal box where she kept her stamps, date-stamp and official forms . . . There are two empty sweetie jars on a shelf; one lies with jagged edges on the counter, fallen.

Many of the village doors have been wrenched off.

Five or six years before, a colony of hippies from the cities settled in the deserted island. They moved into Thomas Vass's two-storied empty house (Thomas Vass had gone with his wife to live in Kirkcaldy) and they lived on National Assistance while they made their poems and pictures and songs. In spring the flower people – a dozen of them – would plant vegetables and dig peats, so they said. One gentle pair had even brought a sack of rice-seed, having heard in the cities of the south that there was much rain in the northern islands and rice grows well in flooded fields . . . A few planned to live on water, wild herbs, and potatoes. That first winter they had no fuel, so they removed doors from the village houses to burn in their open hearth, and had a go at the oak counter in the bar. The ships' timbers that had been the rafters of several houses burned well. But that first severe winter shrank their innocence and their lyricism: Avalon and Tir-nan-Og might not be here, after all. Only the children's faces shone like apples among the snow-flakes, and their eyes glittered like stars . . . By garden-digging time in March, and peat-cutting time in May, most of the hippie families had packed and gone. A half-dozen or so tougher ones lingered on till the onset of the following winter, which was all gales and rainstorms . . .

(It seems that one, at least, might still be in the island. The man has seen smoke drifting across the hillside from the poorest place in Norday, Swinhurst. It was peat smoke. There was a goat in the yard, just as there had been when old Winnie lived there. Could it be? . . . No, it was impossible. Winnie, if she was still alive, would be over a hundred. And how could that delicate grand-daughter have survived wartime in Norday?)

The chill that comes from the doorless smithy is more intense than in the other deserted places. The forge, starved of its fires, is gray and shrunken, and seems to send out cold gules. The anvil that had clanged and tolled for a century is silent. A few horseshoes hang on nails on the wall . . . Here, as well as in the inn, the stories of the island had been told, over and over, until all trivia and irrelevance had been beaten out, and the stuff of legend began to take shape.

'It should not have ended that way,' says Thorfinn Ragnarson. 'I think the saga of the island can never be told now . . . You did well in your day,' he says to the ghosts in the smithy. 'Now be at peace, wherever you are.'

Some of the ghosts may still be wanderers in the wind. Many of them had left Norday with their families at the war's beginning, and moved to Kirkwall or Hamnavoe, or out of Orkney altogether. They had died and been buried in strange places. Matthew Ragnarson and his second wife Tina Lyde had moved to a cottage in Selskay across the Sound. Matthew died in 1944, and his will insisted that he be buried in the kirkyard of Norday among his ancestors. It hadn't been easy, in 1944, getting per-mission for a burial in this embattled island, with fighter planes taking off and landing every hour, and klaxons wailing, and perpetual target-practice over the sea making the cliff birds rise and whirl again and again in clamorous broken rings. But it had been managed, and an RAF chaplain performed the service, with Tina snivelling into her crumpled hankie and the skipper, mate, and engineer of the *Raven*, and Jimmo Greenay, lowering the Selskay-made coffin into the Ragnarson burial plot. (The son and heir, Thorfinn, could not be present: he was then in Stalag 29B in Bavaria, glad enough – in a way – to be left in peace in a world tearing itself apart. The day of the funeral he had been writing with a blunt pencil in a Red Cross pad: a chapter in an ongoing thriller.)

There comes a cry on the wind. At the yard of Swinhurst someone – a woman – is hailing him.

He wants nothing to do with her. What right has she to be in Swinhurst, usurper that she is? How has she clung on to the hillside croft, three years after the other drifters and dreamers have gone? Another winter, and she will have gone, too, surely. Five winters of storm and darkness and solitude would drive anyone mad, if the ancient

197

sustaining dust has not been grained in to the person, body and spirit.

The woman calls again, and beckons him.

He makes a gesture of denial, then turns his back on the stranger and leaves the tranquil village of the dead.

Near the kirkyard gate is a small stone: GEORGE WYLIE, POSTMAN and GRAVEDIGGER 1890–1941 . . . Who buried Geordie Wylie, as the Spitfires took off and landed, defending the naval base of Scapa Flow over the hill? . . . And there too, JACOB OLAFSON 1865– 1930: Thorfinn had sat on the kirkyard wall one day on his way home to Ingle from school, and watched Geordie Wylie digging that grave.

The next forlorn ruin in Norday is the big house, standing there like an eyeless skull. The flower people had not managed to get pickings there – Thomas Vass, before he left, had seen to it that all the windows and doors were shuttered and bolted. But the bolts had rusted and the spars fallen in last winter's gale. The roof is half fallen in. The ancestral hall reeks of decay, in this wind blowing off the shoulder of Fea.

It is time for the story-teller to get back to his hut. His walk through the island has made him hungry. There is nothing to do but boil a few last potatoes and open a tin of bully beef. All his provisions are brought once every week or ten days by a Selskay fisherman, who gets them on his behalf from the Selskay Co-operative: bread, potatoes, tea, sugar, milk, tins of meat and fish. He is half ashamed to exist on that kind of food – it is cheating, and against the spirit of the island . . . Well, in another few weeks he will be eating Norday fish, at least, if all goes well.

He must have another look, soon, to see if there is any

land worth cultivating. The arable land is scabbed with cement and tarmac. The concrete is everywhere – it will not be easy.

Tomorrow or the day after he will try to get *Scallop* into the water. Can he manage by himself? Better wait, perhaps, for Mansie Drever the Selskay fisherman. (He hopes Mansie won't have anything bad to say about his boat-patching. Mansie has a very critical eye.)

There is a tin of sardines and a tin of salmon on the shelf. No: he will not insult his island by eating foreign fish out of a tin. While the tatties boil on top of the stove, he opens a tin of spam. (He hopes that the vanished pigs of Norday will forgive him.)

He can't be sure, either, that the oatcakes and cheese he munches after his spam and tatties are products of Orkney. The tea from the tin mug, certainly not.

He thinks with sudden longing of the ale brewed in half the crofts when he was a boy. The dryness is in more than his throat – his whole body wants that heavy essence of loam and rain and sun. Nothing he has seen anywhere in the world has been so lovely as the barleyfields of Ingle and Glebe and Westvoe undulating in an August sea wind. In Stalag 29B the thought of it had made him weep, more than once. But afterwards, everyone, prisoners and guards alike, had wondered at the sudden happiness of this rather taciturn lazy boy from the islands . . . It never lasted beyond a day, that secret delight. Then he had gone back to his scribbling in the Red Cross notebooks.

*   *   *

The German commandant – a red-faced beer-drinking Bavarian major – had permitted him to send a fair copy of his novel to a publisher in England, via the Red Cross.

Sergeant Evans had conveyed this odd request to the administration office, after telling Private Ragnarson the guards would burn the manuscript in the office stove . . . But no! Major Schneider sent word by Sergeant Evans, the next day, that he wished to see the writer of this scratched and blotted work. And the soldier-author was led by a German guard, in fear and trembling, to the sinister holy of holies. Hitherto he had only seen the commandant occasionally, at a distance, getting in or out of his black staff-car.

Major Schneider had said, 'A romance, eh? This is more sensible than digging dangerous tunnels to escape . . . But, soldier, I think a publisher will only look at such a heap of hand-written sheets – no? – and throw them in his waste-paper basket . . . So, your great masterpiece will be lost forever . . . That will never do . . . Let me think a little . . . Yes, tell your sergeant that I will see him tonight at 7 o'clock prompt, concerning your work of genius. I would not want posterity to blame poor Major Schneider for the loss of a great masterpiece of literature. By no means . . . Boy, wait. You like beer, no? Here is a litre of good Munich beer, in this bottle. Here are two glasses, one for the old soldier-warder, one for the young prisoner-poet . . . You like this beer? I also, I like this beer . . . We will drink to the completion of the romance, whether the publisher in England likes it or not . . . But it cannot be sent in this state, with so many blots and scratchings-out and amendments . . . What is your name, Ragnarson? . . . What is a Norwegian doing in the British army?' He had turned out to be a kind humorous man, Major Schneider. He had never begun to address a prisoner with 'Heil Hitler!' like the other guards. Indeed, the portrait of Hitler on the wall over the major's desk had a slight sideways twist to it, as if in derision.

On the far wall, over his bunk (for his regime was as spartan as the prisoners' he guarded) hung a silver baroque crucifix.

Major Schneider's plan for the novel transpired that evening when Sergeant Evans came into the hut carrying a battered typewriter. He set it on the table in front of Private Ragnarson. 'The old swinehound, the commandant, says you're to be given this. A loan. Take good care of it, my son, otherwise you'll get yourself into a whole heap of trouble. And me, too, most like.'

Private Ragnarson had never struck a typewriter key before. Now he set about the task, slowly and painfully, of transferring the contents of his historical thriller from manuscript to typescript. It was enough to drive his mates mad. In the end Sergeant Evans had him confined to a junk-room close to the barbed wire, and there, for weeks, but with growing confidence, he chattered and stuttered out his book. He typed the last page when the scent of apple blossom came wafting on the wind through the barbed wire.

He wrapped the typescript in brown paper, and scrounged enough string to make a secure parcel.

'I wouldn't bother,' said Sergeant Evans. 'They'll want to read it, of course. Could be secret messages. In any case, sending of parcels out of the camp isn't allowed. Not a hope, I should say. We can but try.' And Sergeant Evans took the sealed parcel away, shaking his head, to the office.

Sergeant Evans was back inside an hour. 'The old swinehound wants to see you instanter in his office. Look sharp, lad. Looks to me you're in deep trouble.'

201

'Ah, the poet,' said Major Schneider. 'Welcome, Nordic poet. It seems to me, there are not enough poets in the world. Plenty of warmen. Few poets.'

Private Ragnarson noticed the portrait of the Führer hung more askew on the wall than before. The German armies were in full retreat after Stalingrad; other German armies were being systematically broken west of the Rhine. (Of course Private Ragnarson knew next to nothing of this, only a few dubious rumours.)

'You drink wine, perhaps? But prefer beer. I also. The last beer we drank together, that was good enough beer. But this beer, here in the jar on my desk, this is a beer with the angel of harvest in it, this is a beer fit only for good soldiers and good poets. You will honour me, my friend, by drinking a jug of this very good beer with me . . .' Then he poured two foaming brown torrents into stone tankards carved deep with coloured mountains and cows, steeples and Alpine cottages. 'It may be, there will be no drinking of such beer for years to come . . .'

When Private Ragnarson had shaken the last amber drops into his mouth – so precious each mouthful seemed, increasingly so, as the beer ebbed in the tankard – the prisoner felt he had never been happier in all his life, not even in the harvest field of Ingle in his childhood. Nor had he felt such friendship for any man – not even his own father or Jock Seatter the blacksmith – as he did now for this enemy officer who kept the key of his prison. A good man; he would have been at home on the smithy bench in Norday of an evening . . . and there he was, refilling the tankards.

'Your romance is despatched,' he said. 'It is on its way to England, through Switzerland of course. May it have great success. May it win for you much fame . . . It will not be long, I think, till you are home again. When the mighty are fallen, and the weapons of war perished. Yes, when those who have lifted up the sword, perish by the sword . . .' And here, if Private Ragnarson was not mistaken, the major turned and looked at the crooked picture of his Führer and commander-in-chief, and shook his head. The major was a little drunk, but now melancholy drunk on a sudden.

'Why do I speak to you like this, boy?' he said. 'I will tell you why I speak to you like this. I also have a son, very much of your age. I *had* a son. He lies dead in Italy, in a place called Monte Cassino, a monastery of peace and prayer that war should never have come near . . . Enough of that. The boy has no grave that is known. He was my only son . . . I hope very much that you will return safe to your island in the north, and live in peace for many years. Let us drink to that, boy.'

This time the bereaved father and the bereaved son (who didn't know as yet that his father was being buried that very afternoon in Norday, among the Spitfires rising and circling) clashed their tankards together.

'Now it seems to me,' said Major Schneider 'that this terrible war will soon be over. Your first romance is written. It may be, you will have time to write the opening chapters of another romance before the guns are silent. The typewriter goes well? You must tell me at once if it gets injured . . . Ah, the ribbon is almost worn through . . . I will have my secretary, Fraulein Krauskopf, look for two new ribbons first thing tomorrow morning. And the thin typing paper – I quite forgot you have to type on coarse paper . . . That somewhat servile Sergeant Evans will bring your ribbons and typing paper tomorrow. And now go, and God be with you, my boy . . .'

'I wouldn't have believed it,' said Sergeant Evans. 'That lazy git Ragnarson comes back from the old swinehound's office sloshed as a tadpole!' . . .

Next morning Private Ragnarson began work on his second thriller, typing straight on to the thin paper . . .

It was a month before the letter came from London – the very day, in fact, that General de Gaulle walked in triumph through the streets of Paris – saying that the publisher liked Mr Ragnarson's novel quite well, and that with a little editing they might feel inclined to put it in their spring list.

For weeks past American bombers in formation had been seen from Stalag 29B, flying north, very high, from Italy, or east from France. One morning when a formation of Yankee bombers flew overhead, Lance-Corporal Wilkins from Wigan had raised his head from the little field where he was planting potatoes, and waved his spade and cheered. The corporal-on-guard, a mild enough man, had ordered Lance-Corporal Wilkins inside, and told the others brusquely to get on with their work. 'They are German airmen,' he said, 'of course.' But Private Loftus from Birmingham, who kept the only book he had ever possessed, *Aircraft Identification*, under his pillow, knew better . . . The morale of the prisoners had never been higher than that day. Why were the German Messerschmitts not shooting the enemy bombers down, over the Alps?

Private Ragnarson's typewriter chattered and clacked away in his little wooden 'house of making'. The romance in progress was about the Scottish War of Independence culminating in the battle of Bannockburn in 1314. It was full of trumpet blasts and snorting war horses, and the crack of skulls under swung maces – blood and thunder stuff . . . His publishers had suggested that the first novel, the navigation of the Dnieper by Norsemen in the Dark Ages, had been too leisurely and lacking in action, though there had been sackings and bear-hunts and Tartar attacks . . . Private Ragnarson showed less excitement than most when the news of the American bombers was whispered through the camp.

He was concerned, though, when one day a long black car drove into the camp and drew up outside the office. Three men in black uniforms got out and went unchallenged into the commandant's apartment. 'The SS,' said Sergeant Evans. Ten minutes later Major Schneider came out, escorted. He was smiling. He raised his hand to the British prisoners, a kind of blessing. The SS officer standing right behind him thrust him into the back seat, and the staff-car drove away at once.

'That's the last we'll see of the old swinehound,' said Sergeant Evans. 'When the SS come with their visiting card, your number's up. A pity in a way. He wasn't a bad old sod, for a Kraut . . .'

That same evening the new commandant arrived: a young captain who hirpled on a stick. 'Wounded in Russia,' said Sergeant Evans. 'So Weinhort tells me. Might be harder times from now on.' (Sergeant Evans and his opposite number Corporal Weinhort frequently exchanged bits of news and gossip, in addition to their official dealings.)

The harder times were already upon them, in the way of smaller rations, and neglect by their captors: the brisk efficiency of the first years after Dunkirk had given way gradually, all the preceding winter, to a certain slackness and carelessness. The prisoners were freer and hungrier. Red Cross parcels arrived less regularly and sometimes

they had been breached and cigarettes and chocolate pil-
fered. Complaints were dismissed with a wave of the
hand: in times of war, Sergeant Evans was told, there
were strains and stresses. Presently things would improve.
But the machine that was Stalag 29B went slower still; it
began to creak and falter.

'Russians on one side, Yanks and English on the other,'
said Sergeant Evans. 'The Huns are caught in the jaws.
Bombers blasting the hell out of their cities too. Mightn't
go too well for us prisoners.'

They saw, sometimes, Captain Weinacker jerking
about the yard on his stick, a young man with suffering
eyes. 'Been through hell, that swinehound,' said Sergeant
Evans. 'So long as he doesn't take it out on us.'

One morning, after his usual meeting with Corporal
Weinhort, the Sergeant barked out, 'Ragnarson, private,
073214, to report to commandant's office 10 a.m.'

'So,' said Captain Weinacker, 'I understand you have
a typewriter belonging to this office in your possession.
You will return it at once.'

Private Ragnarson said that Major Schneider had
allowed him the use of the typewriter for literary purposes. Captain Weinacker looked at him coldly. Private
Ragnarson made so bold as to say that literature knew no
frontiers; it might be the means of binding the nations of
the earth together in peace and friendship, like music and
all the arts. Major Schneider had thought so too.

'Forget Major Schneider,' said the new commandant.
'Major Schneider, in any case, is dead. Let me tell you
something, young man. The time is approaching fast, it
is already upon us, the apocalypse, when all the old values
are consumed in flames. Literature, music, paintings –
all destroyed. The old values. The old religions. The old

206

philosophies. But out of the fires a new world will rise, like the phoenix. A new clean world . . .'

The commandant sat back in his swivel chair – his wounded leg was laid askew on the desk-top. 'You see, I have been licked by the tongue of the dragon already. So, it will not be so bad for me as for you innocent ones – you lambs who sheltered in this pen between the mountains all through the war. What kind of soldiers were you? You should have died like true soldiers in front of the guns . . . *We* are the chosen ones. And still we have only lipped the chalice. We will have to drain it to the last drop . . . But we will do our duty to the end.'

He sat sprawled there, as if a flame had passed through him, and left his face purified.

'You may keep the typewriter,' he said. 'Heil Hitler.'

A guard entered and escorted Private Ragnarson to the barracks.

One morning in April the prisoners woke to find the camp deserted. Some of them had had a disturbed night, for the sound of trucks and lorries and barking Alsatians had gone on till just before dawn. Then the silence fell, and the sun rose over the mountains of Austria.

There was not a soldier in the three watch-towers. The yard was deserted. The commandant's car was not in its place in front of the office. No smoke rose from the kitchen chimney.

The prisoners-of-war cheered. A few of them danced about in the yard. Far to the north, the throb of bombers was almost constant now. 'Lancasters,' said Private Loftus. The prisoners went like wasps through the office block. The Germans had taken everything with them, except a few pieces of furniture. The door to the commandant's office stood open. But for the heavy desk and the portrait of Hitler, the office had been cleared. Sergeant Evans took a drawer from the desk and smashed it against Hitler's face. Fragments of glass tinkled on the floor.

They ate their coarse black bread and drank their acorn coffee, not in a seated company as usual, but each man independently, jostling and getting in each other's way between the stove and the long deal table. Sergeant Evans, for the first time in five years, was having difficulty in controlling them. 'Shut your face, you wet Welsh leek,' said a Cockney soldier who had been very smarmy to Sergeant Evans up to then. Sergeant Evans sent the rebel reeling with a blow on the side of the head. And that, amazingly, had been the first act of violence ever in Stalag 29B, apart from some minor squabbles.

'Get on with your breakfast,' said Sergeant Evans gloomily. 'It's a trick. They'll be back at noon.' He laughed; and nobody had ever heard that strict melancholy man laugh before.

At noon they heard the sound of a convoy of trucks, and the liberators came.

The liberators brought chickens in jelly, joints of cold ham, a hundred loaves of white bread, baskets of peaches and strawberries, tins of cream, jars of ground coffee, boxes of cigarettes and crates of red wine and white wine.

The prisoners ate and drank and most of them got drunk, and a few were more sick than they had been since they had marched on to the troop ships at Dover and Folkestone in 1939.

'We're transferring you behind the lines tonight,' said Major Scheuler from New York. 'Take as little as possible. You'll be well provided. You've stood up pretty well to your long ordeal, I must say.'

Private Ragnarson took his manuscript – King Edward

I of England and his broken army struggling back to England across the Cheviot hills – and his piece of German loot, the typewriter.

*   *   *

Thorfinn has lit the old paraffin lamp in the bothy.

He is sitting at the bench tapping at his typewriter. The typed sheets lie among crab shells and bread crusts.

He is sick to death, now, of historical thrillers. He is trying to dredge something rich and strange out of the mythical past of the islands – the selkies who shed their coats on the moon-blanched sands and danced; the trows who live under the green knolls and love above all the music of men, so that they cajole young fiddlers to their courts inside the hill and keep them there for fifty winters; but the young crofter with the fiddle, having drunk from their silver cup, thinks he has been among the roots and sources for half an hour, no more. And so there is a great mystery in this connection between music and death and time and the food that the earth yields for the nourishment of men . . . It will almost certainly be too difficult for him. Even if it does come off, what will his publisher say about whimsy like this, and his growing company of thriller-hungry readers? It is a seam of rich ore: he will try to mine it, but he doubts he'll succeed.

Meantime the novelist is having trouble with moths. The reckless creatures – a half-dozen of them – are hurling themselves again and again against the lamp-glass, drunk with light. Occasionally one falls, twitching and exhausted, on the bench, but then gathers itself for another mad circling of the lamp, before crashing on to the hot glass, then fluttering and twitching on the bench.

When one of the demented creatures falls into the

209

German typewriter, Thorfinn can put up with it no longer.

Besides, he is tired. The wandering that day among the island ghosts has drained him.

Tomorrow there are the score of lobster creels to be seen to. Tomorrow Mansie Drever will be bringing a week's provisions and a week's mail over from Selskay.

His money is running out. He will have to ask Mansie to take him to Kirkwall, to the bank there. (Mansie will do this, but dourly, for five pounds and a half-bottle of whisky, grumbling most of the way about a good fishing day going to waste: 'The sooner you get that old death-trap of yours into the water . . .') But they usually enjoy their morning in the town, having a pint here and a dram there, and talking to the old men on the pier seat . . .

Thorfinn has asked Mansie the week before about the woman at Swinhurst. 'What woman?' said Mansie. 'I don't know of any woman in your island . . .'

Thorfinn eases the lamp-glass out of the bowl and blows out the flame.

It is dark but there is still a glow in the north-west.

The fog has rolled away silently seawards.

He looks inland, over the island. At Swinhurst, half-way up the hill, there's a glim of light in the window.

He falls asleep at once under his blanket.

Next morning the fog is back thicker than yesterday.

It has washed out Selskay island across the Sound and shorn off the summit of Fea.

He would not know there was sea out there, but for the whisperings, murmurings, washings, bell-cries, random surges, the deep slow melancholy pulse of the ebb.

The *Scallop* is a ghost boat down there beside the rock.

He thinks Mansie Drever won't be crossing from Selskay in a blind haar like this. It is no matter about the letters, but he is really out of potatoes and bread and milk, sugar and salt and tinned meat. He may, after all, have to open one of those cans of fish.

He listens. Jimmo Greenay's alarm clock ticks away on the window-ledge: coming up to eleven o'clock. This is about the time Mansie Drever comes. There is no 'chug-chug' through the grayness.

Well, but there are plenty of things to do – he can do a bit more caulking on the boat – he can wander along the edge of the ebb looking for driftwood, or put blue clusters of mussels into a pail, against the first day's fishing. He can work on the selkie and trow prose poem, but such writing, he feels, is best done by lamplight.

Where, in this blind morning, will the moths be that so scorched themselves against his lamp last night? No weather, this, for moth or butterfly. He can hear a bumble-bee blundering among the ox-eye daisies on a sandstone ledge of cliff just above the bothy. No sack of bee-gold, this bleak day.

But there, suddenly, in mid-Sound, a flash of silver, that is lost almost at once. The sun is trying to cleave the fleece with its sword.

The ebb is making its last gluts far out now, against the skerry.

It is cold, this late summer morning (what would, in the old days, have been harvest-time in the island.)

He hears, listening still, a rattle of stones. The ebb, surely, sifting slimy pebbles far out. But this is a displacement of dry stones. Some creature is moving along the path that goes down from the fields to the shore. There are a few half-wild sheep in the island, and a dog that keeps to the barren end of Norday and must live on rabbits.

The fog lifts and swirls, and there is the woman, shawled, with a sack over her shoulder. The fog hides her again, but her steps are louder still on the loose shore stones, a quarter-mile along the beach.

Shapes loom larger in a thick haar, sounds boom and dwindle.

When he sees her again, she looms like a giantess out of a Celtic legend. Then the haar washes her away completely.

'Go away!' he shouts into the blankness. 'You have no business here. What are you doing in this island at all? The shore belongs to me. I have nothing to say to you . . .' The shore stones roll like thunder.

Now she is there, right beside the door.

She throws the sack at his feet. 'Don't be a fool,' she says. 'Here are a few new potatoes and carrots. And some milk from my goat, here, in this pail.'

'I manage quite well on my own,' he says. 'I'm getting provisions from the store in Selskay this morning.'

It is a voice lost, loved, longed-for (but buried deep in childhood) in this island of the dead.

Fifteen years have honed the bones of Sophie's face to a purer harder line.

'Go away,' he says, confused now. 'I have things to do down here.'

Sophie takes the shawl from her head. Her loose hair is dense with seed pearls.

'Welcome home, poet,' she says.

They spent the rest of the morning together, sitting on the wooden bench outside Jimmo Greenay's bothy, while the sea-haar thickened about them or shredded out into finest tissue, and the Sound was all a fleeting dazzle of sunlight before the fog quenched it, silently, once more. But, in the struggle, the light seemed to be winning.

He told her, in hesitant stumbling phrases – because she urged him (the telling gave him small pleasure) – how he had been since childhood in quest of the grail of poetry, like every man and woman born (but most give up the search soon, in the struggle of getting and spending). He had been fortunate – words were his business; and the hard rock of language, mined and laboured at, might break open and reveal the ore; and out of that gold every poet fashions the chalice sufficient for his offering. (The grail itself is never to be found this side of time.)

*　　*　　*

After the moderate success of the two novels he wrote in Stalag 29B, Ragnarson attempted something more special, a novel that yearned towards poetry, a biography of an islander he remembered from his childhood, the pure inexorable graph from birth to death, but it was a complete failure with the reviewers and the public. Who nowadays is interested in the life of a poor islander, who has been here and there about the world and is not very popular with his neighbours and has no particular insights or skills, and has achieved nothing worthwhile? . . . By this time, in the early fifties, Ragnarson was living among a company of artists and writers and musicians in a high warren in Edinburgh. They called themselves 'artists', but how they got any work done at all in all that winter welter of parties, pub-crawls, quarrels, love affairs and jealousies, he never knew. In spite of the many hangovers, he gritted his teeth and did his three-hours-a-day stint.

213

More historical romances. After the navigation of great Russian rivers and a thin Tolstoyan piece about the Scottish Wars of Independence – the historical thrillers he'd written in the prison camp – he wrote about the early Celtic fortress on the island shore that kept the land-hungerers away for generations, and then again about the British navy in the eighteenth century and the war-hunger for men to serve in the great wooden hell-ships, and how they were mostly outwitted by the island men and women. And again, the romances were published and he made enough to live on, eked out with reviewing and miscellaneous journalism . . . Then, when the cheques came in, the round of parties and pub-crawls along Rose Street and the Royal Mile; and poverty again and hangovers.

It was a kind of treadmill existence, and it became wearisome after five or six years. He grew to dislike it, even though he enjoyed the cluster of writers and artists that came and went, with always the loss of an old face or the arrival of someone witty or enchanting or wayward in some new strange mode. There were a few friends he hoped he would never forget.

And then this hack historian had a great breakthrough. He tried something different – the impact on a primitive simple society, close to the elements, of a massive modern technology. He had experienced it at first hand, in his native island, when that pastoral place had been almost overnight changed into a fortress in the months before the Second World War. He embellished the record, of course, and simplified it too, in the writing.

This novel – not historical but throwing a cold shadow into the future – sweated out among empty beer cans and racketing pop music in that Edinburgh garret – that was an immediate success. It seemed to be to everybody's

214

taste. It was no sooner published than it was hurriedly put into paperback, and translated into German and French; and the Americans gave it a new title and a new format; the television people made a serial of it, and it became a textbook for schools all over Britain, and the author was interviewed and pushed, sweating, on to public stages to give readings from it.

What rejoicings there were in that high Edinburgh slum! The first celebration lasted, on and off, for a week. New faces came around that Ragnarson hadn't seen before – some of them he didn't particularly like.

He suddenly found himself a money-lender. 'Till Friday only . . .' 'Till the giro comes at the end of the month, Thorf . . .' 'For God's sake, if I don't get a tenner before 3 o'clock . . .' 'Listen, I know just the place for us, a small island in the west, just the two of us, away from this jungle . . .'

It was time then to go away, to go home, alone.

To make something of what was left . . . There were enough fragments to see his time out, folk memories, legends, the seal people, the trows that loved music and lived under the green hill. But to write that kind of novel, a man needs to be a poet, and the stones he had broken up to then showed no least trace of ore.

'When I wrote that first novel, about the Vikings in Russia, I knew of course that the Volga doesn't flow into the Black Sea, and it was by difficult portage and bribery and cajolery and violence that Rolf Rolfson and his men got themselves launched on the southward-flowing Dnieper at last . . . I made it as accurate as I could, spiked and marinated the story with all manner of authentic detail. It was all there – all but the innocent poetry of the first imagining.

'Similarly with the heroic cadences of King Robert Bruce and his cunning warcraft that midsummer day under Stirling Castle. Hundreds of thankful letters came from castles and crofts all over Scotland, and from Caledonian Societies in Sydney and Chicago . . . Oh, but it was a fake epic, that book. I knew it then – I know it now, even more vividly. The eye of childhood had seen it more truly.'

If he were to return to Norday (he reasoned) it might not be too late to celebrate what was left of 'the glory and the dream'. He had known the island was a desert now; but the spirit of a place is not so easily quenched. If he were to work a few barren acres, sail to the lobsters . . . Then – it was just possible – out of those endless immemorial arduous rituals, the dance might break.

He had set out north at the end of spring.

It had not worked. He was glad he had come home, but the quest was a vain thing now: the glory and the dream were lost beyond recall.

There was silence for a time between the man and the woman.

But the tide had turned, there were more and more shifting patches of light on the sea. Once Selskay appeared, and was lost again. They saw a few seals blundering on to the skerry. A fur silvered, and dulled again.

'I've talked about myself for an hour,' he said. 'Now you must tell me what things have happened to you in the fifteen lost years.'

She said she had nothing to tell him. She had been among the shades, a long time, until Winnie Swona had summoned her back – a letter from a solicitor in Hamnavoe, telling her that the old dead woman had bequeathed Swinhurst to her, lock, stock, and barrel. That had been in February of this present year. When she had stood at the door of Swinhurst with the key in her hand, the snowdrops were showing among the last shreds of snow.

*   *   *

They walked along the island shore in the afternoon. The waves threw glories of light about them. The great fog bank had rolled away westward. They saw Mansie Drever raising creels under the crag. He would not bring mail and provisions to Thorfinn so long as the woman was there.

'I won't go on much longer with this writing,' he said. 'Till the bread and fish are assured, here I'll sit every lamplit night, toiling at the unattainable poem. In the end the pages will be food for moth and rust.'

'I'll dig my three acres and milk my goat,' said Sophie. 'I'll settle for that. We never find what we set our hearts on. We ought to be glad of that.'

A wave, thrusting higher, washed her feet till they shone.

'It is our son who will be the poet,' she said, as on they walked beside the ocean of the end and the beginning.